'The mental, physical and spiritual benefits of gardening are well known but often overlooked. This beautifully written and illustrated book of stories, prayers and reflections will entice its readers outside to dig, prune, weed and tend and above all to grow in love and knowledge of the Great Gardener himself.'

Jo Swinney, author and Head of Communications,
A Rocha International

'Richard Littledale's wonderful book is a pure gem. It is beautifully written and illustrated and it is as pungent and nutrient-packed as the soil from which it comes. Littledale's book is deep and yet also joyously catchy. It is about gardens and God, but also about grief and rediscovering hope and purpose when grief has brought us low. It is about God's great commission to us through the lens of gardening and gardens and it encourages us to see God as very close and very near, if only we noticed. Littledale writes with rare skill and subtlety and this book will become a modern-day quirky classic. I can kill a plant just by looking at it, but this book encouraged me to pick up the gardening gloves and get stuck in.'

The Reverend Steven Morris, author

Tales from an Under-gardener

Finding God in the garden

Richard Littledale

Authentic

First published 2021 by Authentic Media Limited,
PO Box 6326, Bletchley, Milton Keynes, MK1 9GG.
authenticmedia.co.uk

British Library Cataloguing in Publication Data
A catalogue record for this book is available from the British Library.
ISBN: 978-1-78893-220-2
978-1-78893-221-9 (e-book)

Cover design by Vivian Hansen
Printed and bound by CPI Group (UK) Ltd, Croydon, CR0 4YY

For Mark and Rachel
who always make the garden sing

Contents

A garden is a lovesome thing, God wot!
Rose plot,
Fringed pool,
Fern'd grot –
The veriest school
Of peace; and yet the fool
Contends that God is not –
Not God! in gardens! when the eve is cool?
Nay, but I have a sign;
'Tis very sure God walks in mine.

'My Garden'
Thomas Edward Brown (1830–97)[1]

God the Gardener

It all began with a garden. That said, our idea of what a garden means may be everything from an artfully constructed Palladian landscape to a patch of lawn beside a front door. Once you start to look at dictionary definitions of the garden, many things emerge. However, the consensus seems to be that it is an area beside a house where various plants are grown. Whilst that bald definition is undoubtedly true, I would want something which reflected a little more of the intent behind that piece of ground. I would want something which reflected on the aspiration and perspiration which brings it about. I suggest the following definition: *A part of the earth which bears the hallmark and fingerprints of the one who made it.*

If we choose this as a definition, then it is not just the beginning of God's story that is a garden but the whole thing. From beginning to end, it tells of preparation, sowing, planting, tending and hopeful expectation. It is an account of costly and painstaking transformation all the way through. Any gardener will tell you that at least one of the reasons they love to garden is so that they might make their mark, albeit a gentle and floral one, on the face of the earth. In this, we are so very like the one who started it all.

'Now the LORD God had planted a garden in the east, in Eden' (Gen. 2:8). Thus begins, quite literally, the oldest story in the book. Interestingly, God plants it but does nothing to tend it. No sooner is the garden planted, teeming with plant life of every kind, than God brings a man (Adam) in to look after it. The rules are few, with the emphasis on making the most of this new environment:

> God blessed them and said to them, 'Be fruitful and increase in number; fill the earth and subdue it. Rule over the fish in the sea and the birds in the sky and over every living creature that moves on the ground.'
>
> *Genesis 1:28*

In the very next verse, Adam is told that every fruit and seed-bearing plant on earth was there to provide for him. We should probably not assume that it had an orchard or a kitchen garden, but he was able to forage for whatever food he needed there.

In the next chapter, we discover that in fact there was one further rule. The occupants of this newly planted garden could help themselves to the fruit of any tree which took their fancy, apart from one tree in the very middle. Aside from that, we know very little about the early life in the garden. Were there long walks in the evening shadows, I wonder? Did they train roses to grow around their door or cut flowers to put on their table? Maybe from time to time they lay on their backs in that lush and perfect grass, looking up through the trees and trying to make pictures from the clouds. We shall never know. God's gardener, who now has a companion, flouts the rules and suffers the consequences. When

God comes walking in the evening shadows, Adam and Eve recoil, hiding their nakedness and shame and cowering out of sight.

Apart from the fact that there was plenty to eat, we shall never know the nature of that perfect garden. No one has lived to pass on a description of the way in which it grew. Maybe there were tall trees and elegant ferns. Maybe there were cascades of water and rocky faces where tiny plants clung in the crevices. Maybe there was lush green grass, as soft to the feet as the thickest shag pile carpet. Maybe it moved through the seasons with ease, passing on the baton of colour effortlessly from winter, to spring, to summer and on into autumn. Maybe there were full beds of vegetables and bushes hanging heavy with opalescent fruit where never a pest came near to nibble or destroy. These details remain a mystery.

The cardinal rule of that first garden had been broken, and the result was banishment. In a touching moment, we are told that God made clothes for Adam and Eve (of which they had never had need hitherto), and then it was time to leave:

> So the LORD God banished him from the Garden of Eden to work the ground from which he had been taken. After he drove the man out, he placed on the east side of the Garden of Eden cherubim and a flaming sword flashing back and forth to guard the way to the tree of life.
>
> *Genesis 3:23,24*

A perfect garden, unseen by any human eye which we have ever known, was no more. From this point onwards, any attempt to bring fruit and flower from the earth would involve hard toil. Adam is warned that the ground from which he was taken would:

> produce thorns and thistles for you, and you will eat the plants of the field. By the sweat of your brow you will eat your food until you return to the ground . . .
>
> *Genesis 3:18,19*

The perfect garden was gone. From now on, gardening would be done only ever in adversity. If there was to be gardening at all, then it would be a struggle as it had never been before.

The idea of the garden remained, though. That idea of a place where things grew in a way which adorned the earth and brought gladness to the hearts of those who lived on it would never go away. It lingered, like some distant folk memory passed down from the ancestors who had walked there. When the people laboured in Egypt, cruelly oppressed by their masters, God had not forgotten them. He promised to them a land of their own where they could plant gardens and grow crops in safety and peace. This would be not just a land of 'milk and honey' but a place where their gardens would grow and flourish:

> Like valleys they spread out, like gardens beside a river, like aloes planted by the LORD, like cedars beside the waters. Water will flow from their buckets; their seed will have abundant water.
>
> *Numbers 24:6,7*

The Promised Land would have something of the Garden about it – a place where they could make their mark upon the earth like those who belonged there, and it in turn would bless them with abundance of every kind. I wonder whether they carried seeds in their pockets and saddlebags when they crossed over the Red Sea? Maybe making the seed of their oppressors grow in the land of freedom would have been a kind of justice. Tilling their own earth and choosing their own crops and waiting for sun and rain to fall on their own land might have undone some of the damage which centuries of slavery and oppression had ingrained in their souls. Cultivation and freedom would be inextricably and wonderfully linked for them.

Of course, the freedom did not last. The time would come when the shadow of the Babylonian Empire would fall across the whole of the Ancient Near East. People living in the Promised Land had to abandon their gardens and crops as they were carried away into exile. Those who thought that it would be a short stay were sorely mistaken. It must have been a shock when the prophet Jeremiah wrote to them and told them to 'Build houses and settle down; plant gardens and eat what they produce' (Jer. 29:5). Surely these were the actions of those who never expected to leave? In fact, their time would come, and Amos couched the vision of their return in homely terms. He told them that they would return to the Promised Land where they would 'make gardens and eat their fruit' (Amos 9:14). The Garden was the dream of home.

When the people returned from exile, homes, cities and temple were all in disrepair. Interestingly, the vision of a restored temple given to

Ezekiel had a garden twist to it. When all was well with the temple, and a river of water flowed out from underneath the altar to refresh the desert, trees would grow to this side and that, whose fruit would not fail and whose leaves would be 'for the healing of the nations'. It was Ezekiel, too, who received the promise that the desolate land would become 'like the garden of Eden' (Ezek. 36:35). God, who planted that first garden, had not abandoned his plans just yet. As I have started to learn more about gardening, I have often read of a particular technique to mark out a garden which is yet to be. A plastic bottle is filled with sand, and then a hole pierced in the lid. A fine trail of sand can then be dispensed on the untouched grass or earth to mark the outline of what will flourish there one day. Like a landscape gardener marking out the shape of beds yet to be dug and planted, God had a plan.

Through the Old Testament, like a root system running beneath a lawn, runs the cherished idea of Israel as a lush, fruitful, enduring vine. God looks upon his people as a plant carefully chosen for the best spot in his garden. Not only that but the ground has been cleared of stones and the soil prepared in every which way. I saw this demonstrated during my travels in Jordan. Much of the land is barren, especially in the hottest months of the year. From the road, you can easily pick out a patch of ground for which someone has aspirations. All the stones have been cleared, the dusty earth has been broken up to wait for the rains, and often a low wall has been erected around it. God looks at his vine much as a contemporary gardener might look at their prize rose. He wills it on, looks for every sign of progress and dreams of the day when its grapes will be tasted. Isaiah describes it like this:

I will sing for the one I love a song about his vineyard: my loved one had a vineyard on a fertile hillside. He dug it up and cleared it of stones and planted it with the choicest vines. He built a watch-tower in it and cut out a winepress as well. Then he looked for a crop of good grapes, but it yielded only bad fruit.

Isaiah 5:1,2

Sadly, that day never comes. The vine is rebellious and fruitless, and the aspirations for it are never realised.

By the time Jesus came along, the aspiration was still there, but the reality was something altogether different. The choice vine was sick, and in an occupied land every promise associated with it was hidden as if choked off by the weeds. When I started to clear my garden, I discovered a plant which I did not know was there. It was overshadowed by the laurel above it, strangled by an ivy twisted around it and hidden by brambles growing beneath it. In fact, it is a magnificent phormium – its sword-like leaves thrusting almost a metre up into the clear space it now occupies. Until then, though, it might just as well not have been there.

The land in which Jesus lived and breathed and walked and talked, telling his stories and working his miracles, was scarcely recognisable as the land of promise with its lush gardens and its days of ease. When the end came for Jesus, and he walked out of the city of Jerusalem to the Garden of Gethsemane, he would have walked through a city gate with a tumbling vine carved across its lintel. It was supposed to represent the fruitfulness and health of God's people. The dream was there but the reality was not.

With Jesus gone, the disciples were dispersed across the known world to 'plant seed' of a different kind. Wherever the gospel flourished, it would bear fruit in each changed life. Paul, an early recipient of that gospel, would talk about the 'spiritual fruit' in the life of each believer (Gal. 5:22). All the same, the idea of the garden had not been entirely internalised. To John, exiled on the Isle of Patmos, a vision was given of how the story that started with the Garden would end. One day there would be a city – its beauty almost too intense to describe. Its streets would shine, and its gates would swing open to admit all who had bowed the knee to Jesus. The streets of the city, it would seem, would be more like tree-lined boulevards. Growing on the banks of the river that flowed through the city would be 'the tree of Life'.

> Then the angel showed me the river of the water of life, as clear as crystal, flowing from the throne of God and of the Lamb down the middle of the great street of the city. On each side of the river stood the tree of life, bearing twelve crops of fruit, yielding its fruit every month. And the leaves of the tree are for the healing of the nations.
>
> *Revelation 22:1,2*

The story which started with a garden will end with one too. A good gardener never gives up, and when complete it will, as our definition said, *bear the hallmark and fingerprints of the one who made it.*

Richard the Under-gardener

God being the gardener was all very well. As demonstrated in the previous chapter, the theological cord which ties God to the earth is a many-stranded one. The motif of God as gardener is established beyond all doubt. As we have seen, there is a rich thread running all the way through from the garden of Eden to the tree-lined streets of the New Jerusalem. Through it all, God is the patient gardener – sowing, tending, anticipating and cultivating. That said, the fact that he is a gardener does not mean that I am obliged to copy him. He is a shepherd and a king, too, and I am not expecting to be either of those things any time soon. Not only that, but I have never had any inclination to garden.

In the chapter 'Hidden Threads' you will encounter a plant nursery. It was just up the road from a bakery run by the improbably named Mr Christmas. I loved that bakery. I loved its warm wooden shelves infused with the smell of freshly baked bread. I loved the trays of cakes and buns from which we would occasionally pick. However, the nursery I did not love. In my childhood memory, which I am sure is false, it was always raining there. My parents, who were avid and gifted gardeners, loved to stop there whenever they could, but it was not a love in which I could share.

It was a love which they had developed over the years, ever since they moved into a brand-new house with a bare patch of clay front and back. Starting with the delivery of lorryloads of topsoil, they set about transforming it. By the time I can remember, there was a well-tended lawn at the back, with established shrubs to right and left. Running alongside the garden path were redcurrant bushes, with alpine strawberries planted underneath. These tiny fruits were like little gems – bursting with flavour. The greenhouse, heated in winter and painted with a flour and water paste to shade it in summer, was a nursery for all sorts of seedlings and plants and yielded a crop of delicious 'tiger' tomatoes each summer. By both front and back doors were honeysuckles – their heady scent drifting in through the windows on summer evenings. The front garden had roses and lavender and potentillas, and also a gorgeous pink cherry tree that acted like a beacon every time I came home.

Such were the gardening skills and enthusiasm of my parents that the garden in itself was not enough. My father had an allotment which he lovingly tended. He was tremendously skilled at it all and grew row upon row of blackcurrants, redcurrants and gooseberries, together with rhubarb and other things. I still remember one year when the crop was so great that we sold some to a local greengrocer!

I would occasionally help my father on the allotment. In truth I am not sure how much help I really was. I was usually coaxed by the prospect of a drink together afterwards. However, I used to dread an occasional visit to the fertiliser store. It was full of older men who would greet me indulgently whenever I trailed in behind my dad. He and they would have lengthy conversations about what was growing and what wasn't, whilst all the while I edged closer to the door to get away from the smell of the bonemeal and other ghastly combinations such as 'blood, fish and bone'.

Away from the garden and the allotment, my brother and I were usually charged with the washing up after Sunday lunch. This was fair enough, since we rarely did it the rest of the week. However, this was also the time when *Gardeners' Question Time* was on the radio. My brother and I would exchange glances and snigger when earnest callers rang in to talk about the state of their hollyhocks or where precisely to scatter their 'blood, fish and bone'.

Years on, and married with children, the gardens in our first two houses pretty much had to look after themselves. Our second manse was situated at the top of a steep chalk escarpment, so I always kept an eye on the state of the fence, lest any of the children should wander through and disappear. It had pear and plum trees, which yielded lots of fruit each year. There was also an apple tree in the middle of the garden that would sprout spectacular clumps of mistletoe every winter. They made for great Christmas decorations, and I would often give bunches to others who wanted to dress their houses up. Down the side of the house was a pathway completely overgrown by bushes, brambles and creepers. One year I went out to tackle it on the afternoon of the Wimbledon ladies' final, which my wife was watching in the lounge at the time. When I finally broke through the brambles and poked my head through the open window with the words 'Dr Livingstone, I presume,' she laughed and laughed.

The next house had a smaller garden, and any work in it was kept to the strictly necessary. I got rid of the front lawn and replaced it with gravel so that I didn't have to mow it. In the back, I dug up and reseeded the lawn in an attempt to undo the damage of years of football. This was not a successful enterprise. It took a whole day to dig it over, which meant that by the time I came to rake it flat, I was too tired to do it properly and failed to level it. After what seemed like weeks of crossing a replica of the Somme on duckboards to get to the washing line, the shoots began to come up. They were bright and green – but the lawn was more bumpy and uneven than it had ever been.

Apart from that, I harvested the blackberries each year and occasionally hacked at the weeds and brambles when they encroached too far onto what passed for the lawn. There were two brief bursts of enthusiasm. In the first, I dug out what had once been an old pond. I threw away the concrete frog with a spout in his mouth, rearranged the boulders and constructed a rock garden of sorts. I mixed compost and grit to place around my newly laid rocks and planted hardy alpines in the ridges and furrows I had created. Unfortunately, they were not quite hardy enough to withstand my regime of neglect. Before too long, the rock garden looked as lifeless as the pond had done before it.

My other foray into gardening was an overgrown flowerbed just outside the back windows of the sitting room. The collection of brambles and straggly ornamental grasses was long past its best. I ripped it all out and started again with a heather bed, whose story you can read later on. It looked good for a while, but my enthusiasm was short-lived and stretched only so far as trimming the heathers occasionally and pulling out the weeds which poked up through them. Gardening, for me, was a reluctant fight with rebellious weeds, which they easily won on account of my indifference.

That is how it would stay for many years, until the late spring of 2019. By then, I had been widowed and living alone for almost two years. That laughter over the Dr Livingstone joke was long gone and so many other happy memories with it. I found that the winter evenings were not too bad. With the world dark outside, it was possible to make the house cosy and find distraction. As the days lengthened, though, it was a different matter. A house with windows open to the warm air seemed so much bigger and lonelier without her.

Other people sought refuge in their gardens, but mine just made me feel ashamed. Three years previously, the church had sent a working party to clear and tidy it in order to welcome their new minister and his wife. Now she was gone and so was the tidiness. The twisted brambles and encroaching weeds on the outside reflected something of my state on the inside. Why wouldn't a man who felt like this have a garden like that? After a visit from some friends (which you can read about later), I took a very deep breath and started to work on this outside space of mine. There was so much to do, and I loved it.

As the evenings got longer, so my time in the garden got longer too. I would often be out there all the way through until the light faded at the end of the day. The dog would come out and join me to start with, lying down beside me or pushing an inquisitive wet nose into my ear as I knelt to plant something new. She soon got bored, though, and retired to a sofa indoors to leave me to it. I would work on alone, never feeling lonely with the birdsong and the glow of the setting sun for company. Even when I came in, I would find myself eagerly planning the next bit of the garden to tackle over a bedtime drink. All of this was very healing to me. Bereavement can feel like something which is done 'to' you, or at least happens 'to' you. When you begin to shape and tend a garden, placing that all-important fingerprint upon it, you are gaining a little control. You are becoming an actor in your environment, rather than merely an occupant within it.

A few months in, I was discussing some of this with a friend of mine over coffee. I was describing how good the gardening made me feel and how much difference it made to me. That particular friend is a skilled and experienced counsellor. She nodded sagely and said that what I was describing was in fact ecotherapy. She went on to describe some of the benefits I was experiencing, from the scent of the newly turned soil to the joy of tending growth, to the good sleep born of physical, rather than emotional, tiredness. All this is nothing new, it would seem. During the nineteenth century, it was often noted that patients who had to work outside in the grounds and gardens, to pay for their care, fared better than those who did not. GPs and other health professionals often include gardening in social prescribing on account of its long-term benefits.

For me, what had started as a kind of ecotherapy became more *eco-theology*. Through this partnership between inept and unskilled creature (me) and bountiful creator (God), I was reflecting on aspects of my faith which had never struck me before. They are aspects which you will find in the chapters which follow. Some of that reflection was around the axis of sovereignty and responsibility. I believe God to be sovereign, and yet I labour to do whatever I can in the time which is given to me. This is a piece of theology writ large in the act of gardening – where we prepare the soil and sow the seed in faith, but God provides the true magic of growth and bud.

Not only this, but a work ethic which shaped my daily life as a pastor was being reinforced in the act of gardening too. I believe passionately that the work of the kingdom is a divine–human partnership. From him it requires guidance and blessing, and from me it requires both hard work and faith. To come in from a long session in the garden with blisters and a stiff back was to have that belief affirmed all over again. Looking out hopefully across earth that I had worked at cost and hoping for growth was an act of faith – a bit like looking out across my church. This was starting to feel like theology written on flesh and bone in sweat, rather than theology written on paper or screen.

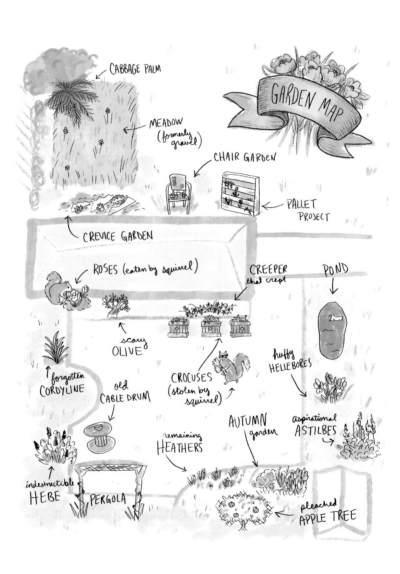

CABBAGE PALM

MEADOW
(formerly gravel)

GARDEN MAP

CHAIR GARDEN

PALLET PROJECT

CREVICE GARDEN

ROSES (eaten by squirrel)

CREEPER that crept

POND

scary OLIVE

↑ forgotten CORDYLINE

old CABLE DRUM

CROCUSES (stolen by squirrel)

huffy HELLEBORES

remaining HEATHERS

AUTUMN garden

aspirational ASTILBES

indestructible HEBE

PERGOLA

pleached APPLE TREE

How to Use This Book

If I could invite you all round, in person, to share my garden, then I would do it. We might run our fingers through the feathery tops of the ornamental grasses or look at the miniature world of the succulents. We might pick out the splashes of colour in the long grass of the little meadow, or savour the heady scent of the jasmine in summer. I'm sure a cuppa would be involved somewhere, and we would sit and savour it as the scents and sounds of the garden made their way over the rim of our mugs.

Sadly, that is not possible – so I have opted for the next best thing. Consider the next fifty-two chapters as an extended invitation to enjoy the garden with me. You visit it in a state of incompletion, as you do with any garden. You will read about failures as well as successes, about the plants which perished as well as the ones which flourished. Along the way, you will meet the creatures and plants which occupy this space with me. More than anything, I hope that they will be your teachers, as they have been mine. They have taught me many lessons about patience, humility, hope, fruitfulness and the abiding goodness of God.

Fifty-two chapters sounds like an awfully long garden visit. By the time you have read them all, the tea or coffee in your mug will have long gone cold. My suggestion would be that you take these next chapters one at a time – pausing to reflect as you might pause to cup a peony bloom in your hands or to smell a rose. Gardens and hurry are poor companions, I find.

Before you push open that garden gate, I should maybe explain a term to you – 'project garden'. Lots of people's gardens have names with a hint of poetry in them: 'silver meadows', 'tall trees' or 'sycamore grove'. Mine has the rather more prosaic 'project garden'. The thing is, I love a project. I love to have something on the go which demands my attention and uses my energy and makes me dream. 'Project garden' has been just that and continues to be. I have a sneaking suspicion that there is an equal and opposite 'project Richard', organised by the Gardener – but you will have to make up your own minds about that.

Tale 1

Hidden Threads

The tick, tick of the indicators as the car turned off the main road brought a silent groan from the passengers in the back – my brother and me. Once again, we had paused on the route to my Granny's house to stop off at a nursery. I remember being very confused the first time it was mentioned and wondering where all the children could be. It was not that kind of nursery, of course. It was the other kind.

This was a serious plantsman's nursery. This was not a garden centre with glossy books, kitchen utensils and quirky gifts. This was a nursery. There was a white house (into which nobody went), a collection of greenhouses and row upon row upon row of plants. There were big plants and small plants. There were green plants and flowering plants. There were vegetables and trees and all sorts in-between. My parents would walk up and down the rows like children in a sweet shop, picking up a plant here and a plant there. Sometimes they would double back to swap one for another. All the time, my brother and I would trail behind, trying our best not to let our mounting boredom get the better of us.

Once home from our visit to Granny's, the plants would be unloaded with a degree of reverence and usually given 'a good long drink' before planting the next day. As you can probably tell, the whole process left me cold. I did enjoy the benefits of the garden. I enjoyed the alpine strawberries grown along the fence next to the washing line. I enjoyed the tomatoes grown in the greenhouse – especially the 'tiger' ones with their stripes. I loved the smell of the honeysuckle which tumbled ever closer to the back door, and I loved to watch the bees come and go across the mounds of white and purple heather.

Occasionally, and very reluctantly, I would take my turn at mowing the lawn – but my heart was not in it. As you have read, my efforts as an adult were little better. Aside from some lacklustre lawn maintenance and a stab at rock gardening, there was nothing much. The only small flash of success was the heather bed, which you will encounter again in 'Ericaceous Error'.

Sometimes God is weaving threads into our lives whose purpose we simply cannot see at the time. It may be because we don't want to, but then again it could be because he does not intend us to. They are not for seeing right now – they are part of an overall design whose wonder and complexity we could never imagine. The God who 'works for the good of those who love him' (Rom. 8:28) had something in mind in those far-off trips to the nursery – though I never knew it.

Bible Reflection on Genesis 50:15–21

The Old Testament story of Joseph has it all – family rivalries, imprisonment, wealth, power, jealousy and death. On the very last page of the story, there is a final cliff-hanger. Joseph's brothers are now living with him in Egypt, having patched up the rivalries which once drove them apart. Now, though, their father and protector, Jacob, has died – and they worry that terrible things might happen. Joseph, who is now a very powerful man, reassures his brothers:

> You intended to harm me, but God intended it for good to accomplish what is now being done, the saving of many lives.
>
> *Genesis 50:20*

There are things going on in your life right now which you cannot understand. They may seem puzzling, troubling, or even downright sinister. Remember, though, that God has the bigger picture. Right now, he can see how the threads of your life, even this one, are being woven into a tapestry yet to be unveiled. It is not to be seen now, maybe, and not even tomorrow – but one day.

Pause for Prayer

This is a good moment for an honesty stop: an opportunity to tell God about those things going on right now in your life which you are really not enjoying. Don't hold back, but rather tell him in all the gory detail. When you have done that, just pause and sit quietly in his presence . . .

Dear God, if I claimed to understand why these things are going on right now, I would fool no one, and least of all, you. Instead, I have simply described them to you. Like a child taking an adult's hand to cross a busy road – I shall trust you with these things for now. In faith, I ask that one day I might see what it has all been for. Amen.

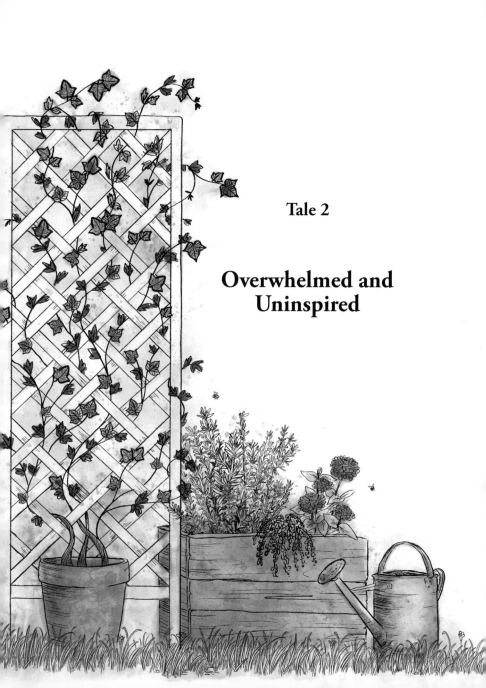

Tale 2

Overwhelmed and Uninspired

There are no two ways about it – this was a bad day. Earlier that week, I had been to the cemetery to visit the spot where my beloved wife, Fiona, was laid to rest. Over her grave grew the pink cherry tree which I had chosen specially. For the second time in a row, an ornament which I had placed on the tree had been stolen. It wasn't a valuable thing – but the fact that it had been stolen really tugged at my heartstrings. Why would anybody do such a thing? Now, I was at home and staring at the dreaded bench.

The bench had been a Christmas present some years ago, and on moving day, we had placed it under a pergola at the bottom of the garden. The intention was that, when summer came, we would sit on it together to enjoy the setting sun. It never happened. Fiona got too sick to leave the house, except for vital things – and the bench was forgotten. Now I looked at it, a widower, and sighed as I saw the weeds growing up and over and through it. They seemed to me like a symbol of all the stolen years and failed plans. This bench was not to be sat upon, ever, they seemed to say.

The view to right and left wasn't much better either. To one side was a bed of brambles and weeds, stretching across to a shed and the fence at the bottom of the garden. To the other, swaying weeds were brushing at the base of my washing line. I felt ashamed that the garden, on which teams of volunteers from the church had worked for mine and Fiona's arrival three years before, had been allowed to fall into such neglect. It all felt like a three-dimensional reflection of my own emotional state. A garden should be a space to breathe and enjoy a brush with nature. Mine was more inclined to suffocate with a reminder of what might have been but was not.

It is a feeling I have heard often enough as a pastor. People feel that their lives are so far from the way that God intended them to be, that they do not know where to start. Overwhelmed by the task, they simply put it off for another day – and the weeds grow and grow. What they need is somewhere manageable to start.

That is how it all began for me – a delightful, absorbing hobby, which I would come to refer to as 'project garden'. I walked outside with two people who love their garden, sighed at the mess and asked them where on earth I should start. They talked about clearing a patch at a time – leaving the intentional plants and getting rid of the weeds. As each patch was cleared, they said, I should put down bark to discourage the weeds, and then choose what new plants to add to my new, growing, canvas.

It sounded like the kind of thing which other people do. It sounded like that little word 'just' which trips off the tongue of a DIY enthusiast when describing some project which would scare the life out of me. All the same, I decided to give it a go. After all, it couldn't get any worse.

Bible Reflection on 2 Corinthians 4:7–10

The apostle Paul was a brave man and also an energetic one. The tales of his travels around the Mediterranean leave me breathless, even twenty centuries later. It was not all plain sailing, though. In the city of Corinth, he came closer than he had ever done to giving up. In the end, a voice from God saved the day, but it was a close-run thing. Writing to the people in that city, sometime later, he described with disarming honesty how fragile we all are:

> But we have this treasure in jars of clay to show that this all-surpassing power is from God and not from us. We are hard pressed on every side, but not crushed; perplexed, but not in despair; persecuted, but not abandoned; struck down, but not destroyed. We always carry around in our body the death of Jesus, so that the life of Jesus may also be revealed in our body.

Whatever it is which you feel you must tackle right now, and however big a mountain it might seem, your ability to tackle it is greater than it might appear. Tell God about your weakness, and he will tell you about his strength.

Pause for Prayer

Stop now and take a breath – a deep one. Then let it all out in a puff of the dimensions usually reserved by a toddler for showing their displeasure. God knows all about your limits. In fact, he knows more about them than you do. That said, he loves nothing more than to work through them with you.

Dear God, this job is too big and I am too small. I can see how other people tackle it, and I can admire their efforts. Every time I do that, though, I grow less and less sure of my own abilities. Help me, Lord, to get started. I don't mind about steps 3, or 4, or 10. For now, step 1 would suit me just fine. Amen.

Tale 3

Ericaceous Error

So, that was it, 'project garden' was under way. One dull morning in May 2019, I took the advice I had been given to tackle one bit at a time and chose my first target. It was to be the flowerbed by the shed. I use the term 'bed' loosely. In truth, it was a jagged triangle of brambles which caught my eye every time I looked out of the kitchen window. To the left was a nice new shed – put there by the church when I first moved in. Behind it was a broken green water butt, full of the kind of slime which belongs in a laboratory. The rest was a desolate jungle of weeds.

After a few hours' work, I leant on the handle of my very underused spade and could not believe what I had done. Despite my misgivings, I seemed to have cleared the space, just as my friends had suggested. This wasn't so much 'gardening' as 'clearance', but it was very satisfying. I could now see the fence once hidden by the brambles. The lawn no longer washed back and forth into the bed, like a river bursting its banks. There was soil, actual soil, showing where once the weeds had been. Whatever should I do with it now?

Keen to fill the space, and to bask in the glow, I headed off to the nearest garden centre. I knew just what to plant, as I had planted them before. In fact, they were just about the only thing which I had ever successfully planted – heathers. Remembering how I had done it last time all those years ago, I filled the boot up with plants, horticultural grit and ericaceous compost. (Reader, please note the use of an unaccustomed horticultural term.) Once home, I unloaded the plants and set to work. Remembering my previous escapade more than fifteen years before, I mixed the grit and the compost together before planting my heathers. I

settled them into their new homes, took photos of my achievement and waited to watch them grow.

At first, they did just that, and I always looked out at them from my kitchen with that indulgent fondness we reserve for a first project. The little splashes of colour were a reminder that the task was not beyond me. The thing is, those patches got smaller and smaller. Of the dozen or so heathers I planted, only a handful remain. Basically, they were in the wrong place. I might have grown them before, but that was in a different garden, a different soil and under a different pattern of light. What works in one place will not necessarily work in another.

As a pastor of some thirty years, I really should have known this. Ideas which fly in one church crash and burn in another. They are still good ideas – just as my heathers were good plants – they are just in the wrong place. There is a laziness to assuming that what God blessed once in one place, he will automatically bless in another. The soil is different, you see.

Bible Reflection on 1 Corinthians 9:19–23

Here is the apostle Paul again, explaining to a critical audience why he does not always do the same thing in the same way in different places:

> To the Jews I became like a Jew, to win the Jews. To those under the law I became like one under the law (though I myself am not under the law), so as to win those under the law. To those not having the law I became like one not having the law (though I am not free from God's law but am under Christ's law), so as to win those not having the law. To the weak I became weak, to win the weak. I have become all things to all people so that by all possible means I might save some. I do all this for the sake of the gospel, that I may share in its blessings.
>
> *1 Corinthians 9:20–23*

There is nothing dishonest or disingenuous about this. It is simply an admission that when our commitment to a thing is absolute (in this case, the gospel), our commitment to how we do it may have to be flexible.

Pause for Prayer

Is there some area of your life right now where the heather isn't growing? Is there some project where you have done your absolute best, using all your strength and creativity – but to no avail? Maybe it is time to ask God whether you are doing it wrong.

Dear God, you know I want to be useful. In fact, I want nothing more. It's just that things don't seem to be working as I had hoped right now. Help me to take a calm and fearless look with you beside to guide me. Maybe I need to plant something new. Amen.

Tale 4

A Border Swept Clean

It didn't stop with the heathers. Now that the bed in front of my shed was transformed from jungle into planting 'canvas', I was on a roll. With each new day off, a new segment of the garden would come into my sights. Early in the morning, I would assemble my arsenal for the attack. I didn't own a wheelbarrow at the time, so I had secateurs, a fork, a spade, an old rake and a bucket. I would start in straight away with the secateurs, lopping off as many of the brambles as close to the ground as I could. Once severed, I would drag the old rake through the tangled mess of thorns and pull them out onto the lawn. Once cleared, I would go down a little further, cutting back still more. I never seemed to wear the right clothes and invariably came away with cuts and scratches all down my arms. I never seemed to mind, though. It felt like being 'honourably wounded'. After that, the spade would come out, slicing down as deeply as I could to remove the dreaded bramble roots. Finally, I would work to and fro across the bed, turning over all the soil methodically – until it was a uniform deep brown.

After this, I would sit back in my grubby state and admire my handiwork. Most times, I would have a rejuvenating cup of coffee and then pack myself off to the garden centre. Usually, it was the same pattern – two or three plants, a sack of compost and a sack or two of bark chippings. Carefully, I would plant my newly bought treasures, then tuck compost around them as a mulch with all the tenderness of tucking a sleeping child into bed. With a heave and a sigh, I would then upend my sacks of bark chippings and spread them across the remaining bare soil. With so little knowledge of what I was doing, there was often quite a lot of it, as I never seemed to buy enough plants.

Job done, I used to love peering out of the curtains the next day to admire yet another bit of the garden which 'I' had transformed. Oh, the folly of the new enthusiast! For a start, every gardener knows that the real transformation is not one that they can bring about. Green stems and brown roots get transformed into glorious blooms by something far more clever than a gardener. Not only that, but a garden is never static. All that deliciously turned soil with its added mulch was the perfect environment for my new plants – but also for the weeds. They were at best dormant and at worst enlivened, but they were certainly not absent. A garden bed untended is a weed-fest waiting to happen.

So often people look out at their spiritual lives with the same kind of naïve enthusiasm with which I regarded my new flowerbeds. They assume that this or that area of their lives has been fixed and will never require attention again. They are 'sorted' so far as prayer, or worship, or service are concerned. It is rarely the case. The weeds keep coming back every time your back is turned.

Mind you, dealing with them can have a pleasure all of its own, as we shall learn later.

Bible Reflection on Luke 11

Jesus healed many people of many things. Some were troubled by physical ailments, and others were tormented by darker forces. Talking about this, he described how a life set free from a dark spirit can be vulnerable if something good is not put in its place:

> When an impure spirit comes out of a person, it goes through arid places seeking rest and does not find it. Then it says, 'I will return to the house I left.' When it arrives, it finds the house swept clean and put in order. Then it goes and takes seven other spirits more wicked than itself, and they go in and live there. And the final condition of that person is worse than the first.
>
> *Luke 11:24–26*

When God helps us to tackle bad things in our lives, we need to replace them with good ones. Otherwise, our lives end up a bit like a freshly turned flowerbed – waiting for the weeds to come back.

Pause for Prayer

Is there something you have recently tried to put right in your spiritual life? Maybe you have quashed a negative habit or put an unhealthy relationship to bed. The question now remains as to what will come in its place.

Dear God, I thank you for helping me to sort some things out, I really do. Thank you that some things are back the way they ought to be. I worry, though, about whether they will stay that way. Please help me to keep the weeds at bay and to plant something more positive instead. Amen.

Tale 5

Sowing Sunshine

With 'project garden' just under way, I had a little garden experiment going on much closer to home. A few steps from the back door were two red pots. Although made from plastic, they were designed to look like glazed terracotta, which they did rather well. These two pots contained a priceless treasure. My late wife, Fiona, always loved sunflowers. When life was ebbing away and she was often stooped by the pain, she talked of looking forward to the day when she could stand tall once again in the presence of God 'like the sunflower'. When my family and I decided to mark her lasting legacy with a charity in her name, The Fiona Fund, it was maybe inevitable that a sunflower should be its logo. The flower stands out, proud and yellow, against its black background on the design. On the year when the fund made its first award to an outstanding oncology professional, I was given a packet of sunflower seeds.

It was with much trepidation that I sowed them. Although I had started to plant things now, they were not seeds. I had not planted any seeds since sowing mustard and cress in cotton wool with my children. I followed all the instructions, kept the soil damp and watched . . . When the first tiny shoots showed through, I was thrilled. I took a photo of them with a 5p coin to give an idea of scale. Later, a toy wooden elephant was used for the same purpose. By the time that summer came, they were magnificent beauties, their dinnerplate-like heads towering above me and tracking the path of the sun each day.

Invigorated by this success, when the following spring came, I decided I would try again. One lot of seeds were grown from a 'sunflower bar' – looking like a bar of chocolate. In fact, it was a bar of coconut fibre and compost, with sunflower seeds embedded in it. Week after week, I dutifully stored it on the window ledge in the warmth. I kept it damp and watched for signs of growth. When they came, I watched the seedlings like little children as they grew. Meanwhile, another pack of seeds was sown directly into a pot outside the window. I kept it watered and watched for progress. Amazingly, it came. Right now, the sunflowers that started on my window ledge are outside and blocking some of the sun from coming through! When a breeze catches them, they nod their wide golden heads, like friendly neighbours hoping for a conversation. To seasoned gardeners, I am sure this is no surprise. However, to me, the very thought that a seed no bigger than my fingernail can grow into a plant which stands taller than me is a miracle. It feels like even more of a miracle that I have played some part in this. The golden sunshine of these flowers is not marred by my surprise. In fact, if anything, it is enhanced by it.

I have lost count of the number of prayer meetings I have attended as a Christian. I have heard prayers of every description. I have heard anxious prayers, uncertain whether they will be answered. I have heard urgent prayers, desperate for an answer. I have heard dejected prayers, where the hope of an answer is all but gone. Thankfully, I have also heard many jubilant prayers, where an answer has been given. With the latter, it is hard to avoid the note of surprise, as if you were not really expecting God to answer in the first place. I know that, because I have often prayed them myself.

A prayer unexpectedly answered, like a sunflower unexpectedly blooming, is a thing of beauty and wonder to me.

Bible Reflection on 1 Corinthians 3

The New Testament church was full of big characters. There was Peter, who often seemed to put his foot in it; there was Barnabas, whose name meant 'son of encouragement'; there was Paul, who never quite left his fiery nature behind; and doubtless there were a host of others whose names we will never know. As ever, the danger with big characters is that they develop big followings. Paul was keen that it should not be so:

> What, after all, is Apollos? And what is Paul? Only servants, through whom you came to believe – as the Lord has assigned to each his task. I planted the seed, Apollos watered it, but God has been making it grow. So neither the one who plants nor the one who waters is anything, but only God, who makes things grow. The one who plants and the one who waters have one purpose, and they will each be rewarded according to their own labour. For we are fellow workers in God's service; you are God's field, God's building.
>
> *1 Corinthians 3:5–9*

One of the biggest lessons which gardening is teaching me is that it is God, not me, who makes things grow. This is true in gardens, churches and lives.

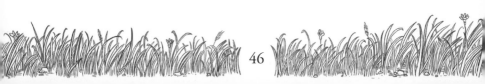

Pause for Prayer

Have you ever found yourself 'believing your own publicity' a little too much? When God gives us gifts of whatever kind, it is so easy to forget where they came from. The taste of success in any field is addictive, and it can readily go to our heads. Now might be a good moment to lay those things down before God, the giver, all over again.

Dear God, I thank you for every gift which you have given to me. I thank you for the skills and the experiences with which you have blessed me. Please help me to remain humbly grateful for them always, I pray. Amen.

Tale 6

Tools for the Job

Meanwhile, at my local DIY and garden shop, I was drawn in by the prospect of a bargain in their sale and headed straight for the tool rack. After all, a gardener should have a good set of tools, surely? Not only that, but a bargain is a bargain – so it was sure to be a good thing. I bought a good-quality trowel; a peculiar weeder, shaped like a claw; and an even more peculiar one with one single prong at the end. It turned out later that it was called a 'daisy grubber' and was of limited use. Not only that, but I felt that a fork was a must. I had one already, but it was rather small. It had been a present from my parents years before and was called a 'border fork'. I had always found it perfectly adequate for the limited amount of gardening I had done – but now I felt that the time had come for something a little more serious.

So, I bought a big fork. The handle was extra-long and the tines as well. It turned out that the handle was a little *too* long, and the tines, being thinner than my old fork, were vulnerable. The first time I used it, I hit a buried root, bent one of the tines and sent a shockwave up my arm which lingered for long enough to put me off that fork for a bit. I still use it occasionally, but mainly I have reverted to the old one. The handle 'fits' me, the tines are still as straight as they ever were, and it seems to do the job better. Meanwhile, the claw-weeder also suffered an unfortunate encounter with a buried root, and the daisy grubber adorns the shed wall since I don't really have any daisies to grub! I should really have bought the tools for the job rather than buying the tools and hoping the job would come along. Surrounding myself with equipment which made me feel like a gardener did not make me one – it just knocked an unnecessary hole in my plant-buying budget.

So often as a pastor I have looked at other churches and quietly envied the staff or the equipment which they have. I have read through their packed programmes with a quiet shake of the head as I realise that I shall never be able to do such things. The point is, though, that I don't have to. If I were to fill my church with other people's programmes, it would be like filling my shed with tools suited to another person's garden. They would look impressive on casual inspection but would be of limited use.

I have not stopped buying tools, of course, but I buy them with a specific purpose in mind. I have bought a scythe especially to cut my meadow grass. I have bought a Japanese tool called a hori-hori trowel to weed around the roots, and at some point I am going to need a rake whose head is not falling off. I shall have to choose which *sort* of rake, though.

Bible Reflection on Romans 12:4–8

The early church was a bit of a crazy enterprise, really. A group of untrained people, whose world had been turned upside down, were given the task of spreading a global message. If they were going to pull it off, then they would need each other and the gifts that each could bring. Look at how the apostle Paul addresses this when he writes to the church in Rome:

> For just as each of us has one body with many members, and these members do not all have the same function, so in Christ we, though many, form one body, and each member belongs to all the others. We have different gifts, according to the grace given to each of us. If your gift is prophesying, then prophesy in accordance with your faith; if it is serving, then serve; if it is teaching, then teach; if it is to encourage, then give encouragement; if it is giving, then give generously; if it is to lead, do it diligently; if it is to show mercy, do it cheerfully.

We have all the tools we need for the job already, just so long as we use them well.

Pause for Prayer

Do you ever feel as though you just can't do the thing you are meant to be doing? There are two possible reasons for that: either you have not discerned that thing correctly, or you need to ask for the tools to do it. God can help with both.

Dear God, I look out at the thing you have asked me to do today, and I'm not sure I can make it happen. Please give me the reassurance and the tools I need to do the job. Amen.

Tale 7

An Excess of Riches

When I moved to my current church, in Berkshire, I was no stranger to the area. I had been born some twenty miles down the road and frequently came to the old market town of Newbury with my parents as a boy. Admittedly, the purpose of our visit was usually a visit to the old butcher's shop on the bridge over the canal – purveyor of fine sausages for generations. However, it was a start. What this meant, though, was that I had a false notion that I knew the area well. I did not. I failed to realise, for instance, that the town lay just on the edge of serious farming countryside. Some of the people with whom I rubbed shoulders when shopping in the town had been farming the land for generations. I was set to find out more.

In my third year of living here, I was invited to take on the role of joint chaplain to the local agricultural society. This was to bring me into the orbit of many who lived and breathed the working of the land. Surprised to find myself as one of their chaplains, I nonetheless felt honoured to serve them. One of my first events was a 'Rogation Sunday' service, blessing the fields and those who work in them, followed by a spectacular farmers' tea. The latter was held in the grounds of an Elizabethan manor house, and I was privileged to be given a personal tour of the exquisite gardens by the person who lived there.

The next time I met her, I told her how much her glorious gardens had inspired my much smaller efforts in 'project garden'. She generously said that she would 'instruct' her gardener to give me some plants. She was as good as her word, and a few weeks later, he gave me an in-depth tour of the gardens he tended, followed by a very generous donation of plants. Maybe seeing the panic in my eyes, he kindly divided them into 'suited to shade' and 'suited to sun' and reminded me of both as I loaded them gingerly into the car.

Back home, I spread out all these riches, gave them a 'really good drink', as my parents used to do, and then . . . quietly panicked. A phone call to a friend of mine, who was working as a groundsman at the time, brought just the help I was looking for. He and his wife came round for the afternoon, and we spent a companionable time placing and starting to plant these new additions. Much of the shape of the garden just now owes a lot to Henry's careful eye and gardener's 'nous'. Without it, a surfeit of riches could have become an embarrassment of wilted plants.

It is a very simple point to make, but we all need help when entering new territory. No one has ever entered the Christian faith with 'prior experience' – since you cannot gain it without stepping in for yourself. This being so, the wise counsel and patient advice of others is of continuing importance. These days, I am often in the position of giving out such advice myself, but I continue to need it too. The garden of my life would soon turn to either jungle or wilderness without it.

Bible Reflection on Exodus 18:17–24

Moses was in a pickle. He was a hero, without a doubt. He had faced down the mighty pharaoh and brought his people out of slavery. Once free, though, they all needed governing. When his father-in-law, Jethro, came to visit him, he saw Moses as a man almost at the end of his tether with all the work he was doing. He handed on some advice:

> Moses' father-in-law replied, 'What you are doing is not good. You and these people who come to you will only wear yourselves out. The work is too heavy for you; you cannot handle it alone. Listen now to me and I will give you some advice, and may God be with you. You must be the people's representative before God and bring their disputes to him. Teach them his decrees and instructions, and show them the way they are to live and how they are to behave. But select capable men from all the people – men who fear God, trustworthy men who hate dishonest gain – and appoint them as officials over thousands, hundreds, fifties and tens. Let them serve as judges for the people at all times, but let them bring every difficult case to you; the simple cases they can decide themselves. That will make your load lighter, because they will share it with you. If you do this and God so commands, you will be able to stand the strain, and all these people will go home satisfied.' Moses listened to his father-in-law and did everything he said.

The advice was good, and Moses lived to fight and govern another day. Sometimes, a bit of good advice at a good time is all we need.

Pause for Prayer

Stop right now and reflect on some area of your life where you do not know what to do. It is sure to be far more important than me with all my plant pots – but you may need to call for help, all the same. Now that you have identified it, why not ask God who might be the person who could help?

Dear God, some days I am daft enough to think that I can do this all by myself. Today is not one of those days. Today, I am asking for your help to identify the person who could advise me, and for courage to approach them about it. Amen.

Tale 8

Of Hogs and Mice

A few years ago, now, two summers before 'project garden' began, I bought a hedgehog house. My wife and I had been watching a programme about natural Britain, and the presenters were appealing for us to provide shelter for these shy and vulnerable creatures. I shopped around, ordered the house and waited for it to arrive. When it did, it came in a gratifyingly large cardboard box. On sliding it out, I was pleased with what I saw. The whole thing looked like a sort of wicker igloo and seemed ideal for the job. I had researched the best location and placed it accordingly, in the shade of a tree and well back from the edge of the lawn.

Several weeks went by and no hedgehog appeared. In the end, I rang the local hedgehog rescue service to see if my little house could be put at the disposal of some needy creature. Apparently, it was not that simple. I would have to negotiate with my neighbours to ensure that there were holes in the fence both sides of each garden to create safe passage for the hedgehog. Not feeling that I could do this simply so that I could enjoy a hedgehog in my garden, I abandoned the idea and left the unoccupied house all alone.

A hard autumn and a hard winter went by, and the little house fell into neglect along with the rest of the garden. When the following spring brought with it my new intent to bring the garden back to life, I decided to relocate the abandoned house somewhere else, in the hope of greater success. When I picked it up to move it, I was astonished to find that it had not been unoccupied at all. Scattered across its floor were the empty shells of hundreds of nuts and seeds. Showing the photos to a naturalist friend of mine, she said that they were almost certainly evidence of occupation by a wood mouse. I smiled at the thought, glad that someone, at least, had benefited from the little house. Not only that, but the following summer a family of hedgehogs took up residence in the garden and were often to be seen near the house.

How often, I wonder, do we find that a plan which appears to be thwarted has simply been redirected? We see it in the stories of the Old Testament, where great heroes of faith have to go 'round the other way' to get to where God wants them to be. We see it in the New Testament, too, especially when Paul's travels are constantly changed by unexpected circumstances.

I'm not quite sure where my wood mouse fitted into the great scheme of things, but I suspect that the provision of a palatial residence for one winter was more than welcome.

Bible Reflection on Acts 16:6

If ever you have a Bible with maps in the back, they are sure to show Paul's missionary journeys. Their coloured lines criss-cross the map of the Mediterranean like a modern air flights chart. These lines represent the fulfilment of Paul's commission to 'preach the gospel'. Not to put too fine a point on it, he was doing a good thing and found himself on a godly errand. This being so, I have always found the following verse from Acts 16 very surprising:

> Paul and his companions travelled throughout the region of Phrygia and Galatia, having been kept by the Holy Spirit from preaching the word in the province of Asia.

Why would the Holy Spirit keep them from preaching the Word of God in the Roman province of Asia? Was he not in favour of such things? Of course, he was. God has a time and place for such things though – and this was not it.

Pause for Prayer

Think back to a plan or aspiration of yours which worked out completely differently to the way you expected. How do you feel about the end result?

Dear God, I have to confess that things so often work out differently to the way I intended. It's not that they are bad, more that I was expecting a hedgehog and got a mouse! Help me to accept the altered outcomes from your hands, even today. Amen.

Tale 9

Take and Eat

You don't have to watch many TV gardening shows before someone will say to the garden designer or expert that they want to encourage more wildlife into their garden. To have this proximity to nature right outside our door is important to many of us. As you know from the previous chapter, I wanted to have that wildlife even before I started on 'project garden'. Within my first few weeks of the project, I was amazed to see the birdlife 'waking up'. A few occasional blue tits had been joined by great tits and their long-tailed cousins with their dusky pink plumage. Each time I worked in the garden, a robin would be close by – just waiting for me to move so that it could check the newly turned earth for worms and bugs. Often, I had only to move a few steps before it swooped down to start working its way across the flowerbed. Within two or three months, a quiet garden had become a delightfully noisy one. However, there was more to come.

I paid a summer visit to some friends in a village on the Wiltshire border, whose cottage garden was a wonderland of flowers, bees and birdlife. It seemed as if every tree had a bird feeder hanging from it to provide an avian larder. There were even a couple of feeders stuffed with dog hair to help with nesting. On my way home, I bought a few more feeders of my own and added them to the garden. After that, I discovered recipes for making garden 'bird-cakes' with suet, peanut butter and lard, combined with fruits and nuts. They were the easiest thing in the world to make and, after a night in the freezer, they were ready to go. Not surprisingly, I was keen to see if my cooking met with the birds' approval. I had a long time to wait. The same thing happened when I bought an old pewter dish and nestled it in the front garden under my window. I half-filled it with gravel, installed a large pebble at the edge so that a smaller bird could stand on it, filled it with healthy rainwater, and . . . nobody came.

I have to confess to feeling a little disgruntled. Did these birds not know what was good for them? Did they not appreciate the effort I had put in? Of course, neither of those things are true. Garden birds are naturally cautious. They have to be, as predators abound in a domestic garden. There are cats and dogs, as well as larger, predatory birds. If I look out of my window now, I often see a robin on its way to feed. It flies to the fence and eyes the feeder from the left. It then flies past it and settles on the ground to the right of the feeder. It may then fly up to the laurel bush and perform the whole circuit a couple more times before finally coming to feed.

Sometimes, we condition ourselves not to take the good things on offer to us from God even when they are there for the taking. We hear something of this frustration in Isaiah 55:2:

> Why spend money on what is not bread, and your labour on what does not satisfy? Listen, listen to me, and eat what is good, and you will delight in the richest of fare.

God had such good things to offer them – but like my robin hopping from fence to ground, to bush and back again, they just weren't sure. It is a pattern often repeated.

Bible Reflection on John 5:2–9

In the days of Jesus, just outside one of the city gates of Jerusalem was a pool with a portico round the edge. Legend had it that whenever an angel stirred up the waters, the first person to reach them would be healed. As such, the pool was a magnet for those in all kinds of need. Here is John's account of Jesus' visit:

> Now there is in Jerusalem near the Sheep Gate a pool, which in Aramaic is called Bethesda and which is surrounded by five covered colonnades. Here a great number of disabled people used to lie – the blind, the lame, the paralysed. One who was there had been an invalid for thirty-eight years. When Jesus saw him lying there and learned that he had been in this condition for a long time, he asked him, 'Do you want to get well?' 'Sir,' the invalid replied, 'I have no one to help me into the pool when the water is stirred. While I am trying to get in, someone else goes down ahead of me.' Then Jesus said to him, 'Get up! Pick up your mat and walk.' At once the man was cured; he picked up his mat and walked.

When the one person in the entire world who could heal him was standing right under his nose, the disabled man could not hear the offer he made. He was so conditioned by his experience that in answer to the question about whether he wanted to be healed, he could only answer that he could not get to the pool in time. His timidity almost made him miss the best offer of his life.

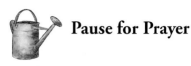 **Pause for Prayer**

Have there been moments, maybe even recently, when you have seen God's offer of blessing or help but have turned away because you were fearful? Maybe, like my robin, you have eyed it up from every angle but then turned tail and fled. Today is a good day to look at that offer again.

Dear God, I know you are always good, and the things you offer are always good too. Deep down, I am just a little afraid, though. Please help me to find more courage today. Amen.

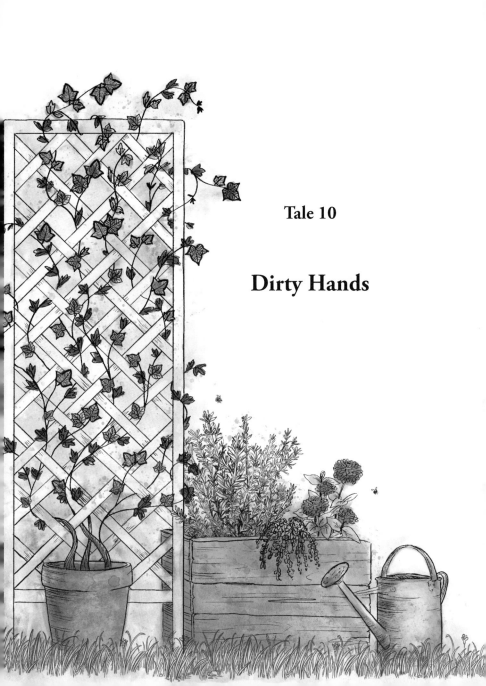

Tale 10

Dirty Hands

Years before 'project garden' began, I used to occasionally help my dad on his allotment, as you now know. You also know that it was done rather reluctantly, and I have confessed how little help I was. I often enjoyed the drink we had together afterwards, and I was fascinated by the farmyard which sat below the edge of the plot. Often, whilst I was supposed to be picking blackcurrants or chopping back weeds, I would get distracted by the goings-on down below. A squealing pig or a spluttering Land Rover was all it took to distract me from the dreaded weeding. After all, what could there possibly be to enjoy about such a task?

Years later, I had a 'plot' of my own to think about. As I started to clear one bed after another, the need to keep the weeds at bay was ever present. No matter, I thought. Whilst most of my tools were stored in the shed, I always kept a hoe outside. That way, whenever I had five minutes to spare, I could easily work my way round the garden, from left to right, turning over the soil. It was a soothing thing to do and had the advantage that it yielded instant results. Looking out an hour or so later, or even when I opened the curtains the next morning, it was deeply satisfying. I had made a difference. However, as any more experienced gardener will tell you, that difference was short-lived. Hoeing only snaps the weeds off at the surface – it doesn't destroy them.

Several months, and one or two gardening books later, I adopted a new technique. I wanted to get to know my garden better – up close and personal. Laborious though it is, most of my weeding is now done on my knees with a hand tool. As often as not, I will use my hori-hori trowel (whose name in Japanese means 'diggy-diggy'). I still work round the garden from left to right, and it still yields results. However, it yields something else too: knowledge. By weeding like this, I get to know the look and feel of every patch of soil. I get to know where the roots lie, where the shadows fall and where the most persistent weed offenders are to be found.

It is something I have continued into my planting too. When I first began all this, I would plant everything using a spade and gardening gloves. I still use the spade, especially for substantial plants, but the gloves have gone. I want to feel the weight of the plant. I want to feel the knots of its roots. I want to snap one or two of them before I sink it into the ground in order to encourage it to grow. When it goes into the hole which will be its new home, I want to firm it in with my fingertips, so that I know it is settled. To me, a good gardening session is one where I need the scrubbing brush afterwards. Dirty fingernails are a badge of honour!

It has always struck me that humankind is the one bit of creation which God makes by hand. Everything else springs to life at the word of his mouth, but we are made by dirty hands. In the account of creation in Genesis, God scoops up some soil into his hands, moulds it into the shape of a human and then breathes life into it. We are the original 'hand-made'. I wonder whether he washed his hands afterwards?

Bible Reflection on Isaiah 60:20,21

Throughout the Bible, and especially the Old Testament, there is something of the meticulous and thoughtful gardener about the way God addresses his people. They are the work of his hands, and as such, they seem to cause him pride and sorrow in equal measure. Consider these words from the prophet Isaiah, for example:

> Your sun will never set again, and your moon will wane no more; the LORD will be your everlasting light, and your days of sorrow will end. Then all your people will be righteous and they will possess the land for ever. They are the shoot I have planted, the work of my hands, for the display of my splendour.

What a thing, to have been planted by God. And what a thing, too, to waste such a heritage!

Pause for Prayer

I tend to feel a little proprietorial about the things I have planted, even though I did very little to make them grow. For the most part, I slid them from the pot in which someone else grew them and planted them in my soil. All the same, I love to watch them grow. Did you ever stop to wonder how God looks at you, as he walks around his garden? What does he see?

Dear God, thank you that you got your hands dirty with me. Thank you that you have never dealt with me at arm's length. I am your planting and the work of your hands. Today, I ask that I might grow, even a little, and make you proud. Amen.

Tale 11

Let it Rain!

Let's face it, rain can be an awful nuisance. If you have a dog, as I do, then staying indoors all day is simply not an option. Four muddy paws and two muddy feet, no matter how hard you try, are not a recipe for a clean and tidy house. A dog which has supposedly been towelled off might not be as dry as you think, which means muddy carpets and muddy furniture all round. That said, I do love the sound of rain. In my view, there is nothing cosier than being warm and snug inside whilst the weather is doing its worst and hammering on the windows outside. For as long as I can remember, my reaction has always been to snuggle down a little further and think, 'I'm glad I'm not out in it.'

I had been working for quite a while on 'project garden' when it happened. It was quite unexpected but deeply significant, as it turned out. It was part way into a particularly dry spell in my first summer as a gardener when I drew the curtains back one morning, saw the sheets of rain coming down, and thought to myself, 'Oh good.' Even as I said it to myself, I was shocked. Had I really become enough of a gardener that, instead of seeing a day spoiled and carpets muddied, I saw the opportunity for something else? Rain penetrates deep into the soil in a way which watering with a hose or can never could. Not only that, but rainwater is free from the chemicals so often found in tap water. A day of steady rain can do the garden an enormous amount of good.

I could have told you that scientifically, years ago. All the same, to feel it emotionally was something else entirely. The whole cycle of preparation, planting and nurturing had become so dear to me that I would happily forego a day of carefree sunshine for the sake of the plants.

It was very strange. Invested in this project as I had become, I really wanted it to flourish.

In fact, I wanted it to flourish so much that I overcame some of my terror of DIY. I bought a brand-new water butt. It took a couple of weeks to arrive, and almost every day during those two weeks, I watched videos online about how to fit it. My main concern was the fact that I would have to slice through a downpipe and instal a 'diverter' to channel the rainwater. Slicing through anything is something which I try to avoid when it comes to DIY. However, despite my fears, it worked. On the day I installed it, I was no sooner in than the heavens opened and the rain came tumbling down. To open the lid of the water butt the next day and see all that harvested rainwater gave me quite a boost.

My years as a pastor have taught me that sometimes the greatest blessings come when the sky darkens and the rain falls. Times without number I have seen people discover new depths to their faith and new facets to God's grace when the going was toughest. The storm clouds come and the rain begins to fall, but soon enough the growth will follow.

Bible Reflection on Philippians 1:19–26

Every time I read anything written by the apostle Paul, I am left thinking how unlike him I am. There is a steel, a courage and a faith there which I would love to emulate, but I have a long way to go. In the letter to the Philippians, he writes from his prison cell and talks of being 'in chains'. All the same, his concern is for them and their faith. Here he talks about his dilemma concerning whether he should stay or go:

> For I know that through your prayers and God's provision of the Spirit of Jesus Christ what has happened to me will turn out for my deliverance. I eagerly expect and hope that I will in no way be ashamed, but will have sufficient courage so that now as always Christ will be exalted in my body, whether by life or by death. For to me, to live is Christ and to die is gain. If I am to go on living in the body, this will mean fruitful labour for me. Yet what shall I choose? I do not know! I am torn between the two: I desire to depart and be with Christ, which is better by far; but it is more necessary for you that I remain in the body. Convinced of this, I know that I will remain, and I will continue with all of you for your progress and joy in the faith, so that through my being with you again your boasting in Christ Jesus will abound on account of me.

It seems as if life and death, blessing and hardship, prison and liberty all sit cheek by jowl for him. Then again, maybe they do for all of us. Like rain on a summer day, God's blessings may fall in unexpected places.

Pause for Prayer

Has rain spoilt your sunny day? Does it look as though your plans are being spoilt? Maybe, just maybe, there could be a blessing in here somewhere. Perhaps, like the summer rain, this might help things to grow?

Dear God, you know this was not what I was expecting. I was looking for sunshine and I see only rain. Help me to believe, and to see, that there is some good in it from you. Amen.

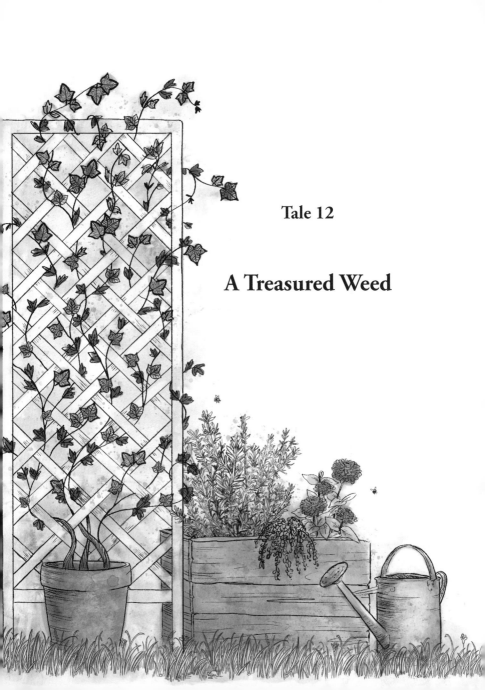

Tale 12

A Treasured Weed

Opposite the church where I work is an antiques emporium. It moved there from elsewhere in town, no doubt for sound business reasons, but at times it feels as if it were put there specifically to tempt me. Times without number, I have wandered in there 'just to have a look' and ended up coming out with some knick-knack or other. On this particular occasion, I didn't even need to enter the shop in order to lighten my pocket. Sitting outside was an old metal trunk, about 1 metre long, with a curved lid and covered in rust. I fell in love with it instantly, negotiated a price, loaded it into the boot (with some difficulty) and brought it home.

With characteristic impatience, I couldn't wait to fill it. I lined the bottom with weed-proof membrane, scattered a layer of gravel on top of that, added a mixture of soil and potting compost, and began to plant. There were geraniums and lobelias, which worked beautifully – tumbling over the edge and looking like they had always been there. There were also some tall verbenas, which would have looked good elsewhere but seemed restricted by the curve of the lid above their colourful heads. Overall, though, the impression was very pleasing. It looked every inch the treasure chest and had a new lease of life. I even took a photo and printed it out for the emporium to show what had become of the old chest. The owner still has it behind his counter today.

When I told a gardener about my success, he nodded with interest and asked me about drainage holes. My face fell. The chest was now full of gravel, compost, soil, and flowers – there was no way I could remove them all. I had foolishly thought my layer of gravel would be sufficient, but he assured me it was not so. 'Put some drainage holes in,' he said, 'as soon as you get home.' A little crestfallen, I hurried home, got out a hammer and nails, and worked my way around the base of the chest. It worked and the plants thrived, but that is not the end of the story.

The following year, this time in a new location, I planted the chest up again. This time, there were no tall verbenas. Instead, there were begonias and busy Lizzies, which thrived. They created a pink and white foam of petals, as if the plants were frothing up out of the treasure chest. The addition of a solar lantern just added to that effect. At night the flowers were lit up like the treasure I regarded them to be. However, unbeknown to me, a weed had taken root somewhere in the bottom of the trunk and found its way out through one of my drainage holes. Without a doubt, it is an imposter. It has no flowers, and it does not belong. I should take a sharp pair of secateurs and cut it off before it attracts even more attention away from the real flowers, but I can't quite bear to. There is something about that defiant little plant's pluck that I admire so much. Somewhere deep down there, in the damp darkness of the trunk, it has sprung to life. Not only that, but it has found a tiny hole through which it can escape into the light and flourish like any other plant. Who am I to cut it off?

The Old Testament often talks about the 'faithful remnant' – the few faithful ones who go on trusting God even when all else fails. They may be small in number, and their voice scarcely heard, but God sees and hears them, always. They cling on to faith – like my little weed clinging on to life – and God honours them for doing so.

I do hope my weed will be back again next year.

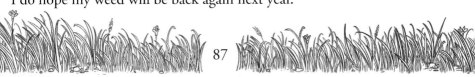

Bible Reflection on Malachi 3:16,17

There are a lot of the passages in the minor prophets of the Old Testament which make for pretty heavy reading. They are heavy either because their meaning is obscure, or because their meaning is plain but hard to swallow. These verses are something of an exception. They come from Malachi – the last book of the Old Testament:

> Then those who feared the LORD talked with each other, and the LORD listened and heard. A scroll of remembrance was written in his presence concerning those who feared the LORD and honoured his name. 'On the day when I act,' says the LORD Almighty, 'they will be my treasured possession.'

In my view, it is worth wading through a lot of the harder passages just to get to this two-word description of God's people: *treasured possession*. It is a lovely thing to be treasured, don't you think?

Pause for Prayer

Thinking of my floral treasure chest, I wonder whether you feel more like the flowers or the weed today? The flowers are pretty, showy and meant to be there. The weed is plain, cheeky and has found its way there. It is so easy to be envious of the attention or the gifts of others, but no good thing ever goes unnoticed by God.

Dear God, will you forgive me on those days when I feel more like the weed than the flower? Some days, I feel like I am a little bit in the way. Today, I ask for your reassurance that I am precious to you, no matter what I may think. Amen.

Tale 13

The Squirrel That Snatched

My grandmother was what you might have called a 'character'. As a young child, I probably thought she had always been old, as children tend to do. It was only as a teenager that I started to hear tales of her younger life. She had been a student at the Slade art school in the 1920s, for instance, and would tell tales of life-drawing classes which made my teenage ears prick with embarrassment. In later life, the garden was her great source of joy and she invested heavily in it. She loved the flowers, the trees, the insects and the wildlife which visited it. Actually, that is not entirely true. There was a particular loathing in her heart for squirrels, who would dig up her bulbs and steal from her bird table. She kept a fully charged stirrup pump by the back door and would dash out and squirt it at them with a speed of which I thought she was incapable. It was quite a sight.

Whatever would she have thought, then, of my squirrel habits? When I first moved into the house, I was very entertained by the antics of the squirrels. They would come tumbling down from a tree next door and skitter across the decking under the kitchen window with a clatter of their tiny, sharp claws. I found this so entertaining that I committed what my grandmother would have regarded as a cardinal sin – and started to feed them. As a keen photographer, this allowed for some spectacular photographs. I knew exactly where the squirrels would be and, often, when – and would get the shot lined up accordingly. On one occasion, I was reviewing a nature book entitled *Autumn*[2] and managed to use the food in such a way that I got the perfect shot of the squirrel apparently examining the book. I was so pleased. Little did I know that I was sowing the seeds of my later downfall.

Once I started to plant things in tubs on my decking, I was keen to see them prosper. I had a gorgeous cordyline, the colour of rhubarb, through which the early sun would shine. I had a tub of petunias, foaming over the edges with their candy stripe colours. I also had a rose. It was a beautiful, pink climbing rose, with a heady scent which would waft in through the open kitchen window. Each day, I would go out and check on it as the buds formed. It became something of a routine to admire them early in the morning. I marked the way they swelled with each passing day, with the outer covering gradually splitting away to reveal the furled pink petals below. One bloom came and then another, releasing their heady scent. That was it, though. After that, each bud would disappear just before the critical moment. On further inspection, each had been neatly severed from the rose by sharp teeth. It was not hard to identify the culprit.

I could almost see my late grandmother wagging her finger. Frankly, I had brought this on myself. That is always a hard admission, isn't it? When things go wrong, we would always rather blame the circumstances or other people before we look to ourselves. I had brought this situation about, whether I liked it or not.

I don't feed the squirrels from the decking any more.

Bible Reflection on Jonah

Jonah was a man plucked from obscurity and given a very distasteful job to do. He was tasked with taking God's message to a group of people who were regarded by many as a lost cause. Jonah was having none of it and made strenuous efforts to run away. One thing led to another, and he ended up being thrown off a boat and sinking down into the sea. As if that weren't enough, he was then swallowed by a large fish. Even there, he still seemed inclined to blame someone else for his woes:

> *You* hurled me into the depths, into the very heart of the seas, and the currents swirled about me; all *your* waves and breakers swept over me.
>
> *Jonah 2:3, emphasis mine*

Jonah came round in the end, though. He came to his senses, cried out for help, got it – and went on with the job. Sometimes it doesn't matter quite so much who made the mess, as long as we get some help clearing it up!

Pause for Prayer

If you asked yourself honestly, right now, I wonder whether there are parts of your life where you have invited trouble, a bit like me coaxing the squirrels onto my decking? Maybe, like me, you have ended up spoiling something which you hold dear. There's no shame in admitting it. In fact, it might just be the first step to putting it right.

Dear God, I'm sorry for those times and places where I have invited trouble in to stay. Please forgive me for the foolish things I have done to make that so. Would you please help me to start putting them right, even today, I pray. Amen.

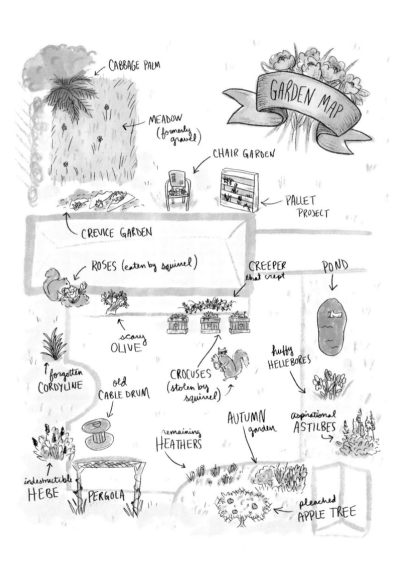

CABBAGE PALM

GARDEN MAP

MEADOW
(formerly gravel)

CHAIR GARDEN

PALLET PROJECT

CREVICE GARDEN

ROSES (eaten by squirrel)

CREEPER that crept

POND

scary OLIVE

↑ forgotten CORDYLINE

old CABLE DRUM

CROCUSES (stolen by squirrel)

huffy HELLEBORES

remaining HEATHERS

AUTUMN garden

aspirational ASTILBES

indestructible HEBE

PERGOLA

pleached APPLE TREE

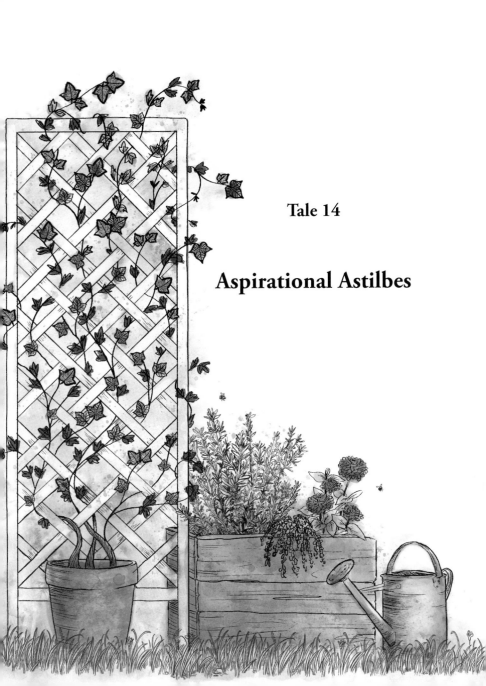

Tale 14

Aspirational Astilbes

'Project garden' had been under way for quite some time now. This new version of myself whom I had not met before was doing all sorts of peculiar things. He was working long hours in the garden until the light faded. He was visiting garden centres with the kind of enthusiasm he had once seen in his parents. Not only that, but he was even visiting gardens on holiday with no persuasion from anybody else! One such was Marwood Hill Garden, in North Devon. Marwood Hill was a labour of love, created by Dr Jimmy Smart in a twenty-acre site tucked into a hidden valley near Barnstaple. Over the years, he had fashioned it and planted it into a vision of sylvan beauty. Through the centre run water gardens, up the sides spread a global collection of tree specimens and in the middle is the National Collection of Astilbe. This is where the problem lay.

Astilbes are shade-loving fern-like flowers with tall, feathery plumes of white, red, pink and magenta flowers. At Marwood Hill they grow by the hundreds, in great waving seas cascading down to the lakes. The slightest summer breeze sends them bobbing in rhythmic waves as far as the eye can see. I visited the gardens twice within a week-long holiday and, on both occasions, visited the nursery shop. On my second visit, a helpful member of staff tried her very hardest to persuade me to take some astilbes home with me. She assured me that they would travel well in the car and that they would be sure to thrive in my shady, woodland corner. I did not believe her. What was the point in trying to emulate such floral perfection, I thought, when I scarcely knew what I was doing? I left the astilbes behind and drove back home.

When the second summer came, and with a little more confidence under my belt, I started to tackle the dappled shade of the bed beneath my trees. Browsing round my local nursery on a quiet day, the member of staff watering inside the greenhouse saw me admiring their astilbes and asked me where I was thinking of planting them. I described the location, which she described as ideal, and bought two on the spot. The next week I bought two more and made sure that I incorporated all four into my daily watering regime. When their leaves started to curl, it seemed like a kind of cruel confirmation that I had been foolish to try. One trip to the nursery and a bit of advice later, they now get extra watering and are thriving.

It is an odd thing, but we are so often put off by the beauty, perfection, or skill of others rather than being inspired by it. My first reaction on seeing Dr Smart's astilbes in their Devon home was to dismiss the faintest notion that I should ever try to grow them in Berkshire. I was wrong. I have been wrong, too, on those occasions when the incredible talent of others makes me more inclined to hide, rather than show, my own.

Next year, I am hoping, if not for a wave, then at least a ripple of pink and white feathery flowers beneath my apple trees. When I see it, I shall bless the name of Jimmy Smart!

Bible Reflection on John 21:15–22

I think it would be fair to say that things were a little 'tense' in the disciples' camp. They had lost Jesus, found him again, were about to lose him once again, and still had in the back of their minds the enormous task that he had given them to do. Read on, as Jesus deals with their frayed nerves:

When they had finished eating, Jesus said to Simon Peter, 'Simon son of John, do you love me more than these?' 'Yes, Lord,' he said, 'you know that I love you.' Jesus said, 'Feed my lambs.' Again Jesus said, 'Simon son of John, do you love me?' He answered, 'Yes, Lord, you know that I love you.' Jesus said, 'Take care of my sheep.' The third time he said to him, 'Simon son of John, do you love me?' Peter was hurt because Jesus asked him the third time, 'Do you love me?' He said, 'Lord, you know all things; you know that I love you.' Jesus said, 'Feed my sheep. Very truly I tell you, when you were younger you dressed yourself and went where you wanted; but when you are old you will stretch out your hands, and someone else will dress you and lead you where you do not want to go.' Jesus said this to indicate the kind of death by which Peter would glorify God. Then he said to him, 'Follow me!' Peter turned and saw that the disciple whom Jesus loved was following them. (This was the one who had leaned back against Jesus at the supper and had said, 'Lord, who is going to betray you?') When Peter saw

him, he asked, 'Lord, what about him?' Jesus answered, 'If I want him to remain alive until I return, what is that to you? You must follow me.'

Even in this wonderful moment of restoration and reinstatement, there is still anxiety about the status and position of others. How quickly admiration is replaced with jealousy.

Pause for Prayer

This might be a good moment to talk to God about those whose gifts you find hard to bear. It's not that you resent others having them. In fact, you have been blessed by them. It is more the fact that their gifts always seem to make you aware of the absence of your own.

Dear God, you know who I am thinking of – and I thank you for their gifts. I truly do. Today, I ask that you might make me inspired by those gifts, rather than intimidated by them. Today, let the flowers you have planted in the garden of my life start to show their colours, I pray. Amen.

Tale 15

The Scary Olive

As you have read through these chapters, you will have realised that 'project garden' is something of an oasis for me. It feeds my mind, stimulates my faith and exercises my body too. On even the hardest or most testing of days, I can find solace there. However, there is one tree which causes me considerable anxiety. I did not choose it and it came to me long before 'project garden' began.

When I arrived in my current church, the final stages of planning my induction service were still being refined. There were certain things which I was very keen to include. One was that the assembled church members and guests should be welcomed by one of the oldest and one of the youngest people in the congregation. This duly happened and was loved by all. Since I was coming to work with people of all ages, I wanted there to be a part of the service which expressed to the children that I was their pastor too. This is how the idea of a 'mini-induction' within the main service was born. A number of the children gathered round me; the wording went like this:

Please will you teach us all about Jesus by telling us lots of stories?

This pot has all our names to remember who we are and that we will listen and learn.

Please will you help us to get to know God as our Father by answering all our questions?

Please take this plant to remember how we want to grow; we promise to ask lots of questions.

Please will you lead us and guide us in the Spirit so that we can learn to have all the fruits of the Spirit?

Please accept this olive tree and its fruit as a reminder of the fruits of the Spirit we will use together.

After that, they presented me with an olive tree, which I can see out of my window right now. To have such a precious thing and to feel responsible for it, and all that it symbolises, felt like quite a burden. What if it were to go the same way as the yellow chrysanthemums you will meet in 'Outdoors Indoors'? Sometimes it almost felt as if it were some kind of horticultural barometer measuring the extent to which I was keeping my promises to those children.

Thankfully the olive progressed well for the first couple of years. Its messy growth in all directions seemed to me like the best kind of symbol of the work with the church's children. The olive was growing just like they were – in unpredictable and wonderful ways. Imagine my dismay, then, when summer saw the tree looking really sick. Despite watering, the leaves had become dry and papery. It only took a strong gust of wind or a bird landing to knock them off. Had I failed? One gardener shook his head and suggested it might be vine weevil. I went to my local garden centre and described the symptoms; the assistant was unconvinced about the pest. She suggested putting it into a really big pot, watering it well and then seeing what happened. I bought just such a pot, took it home and then took a very deep breath before proceeding. I had heard terrible tales about traumatising trees by moving them and this could well be the end of my symbolic olive tree.

Thankfully, it was not. The tree found room to expand in its new home and is flourishing once again. Every time I look at it, I think of the children who gave it to me, and I thank God that they are flourishing in different ways too.

Bible Reflection on Psalm 1:1–3

It is often a mistake to read every portion of the Bible in the same way. Stories are meant to be read as stories, drawing you in. Closely argued text is meant to be read as a logical argument. Other passages are meant to fire our imaginations – like this description of a well-watered tree:

> Blessed is the one who does not walk in step with the wicked or stand in the way that sinners take or sit in the company of mockers, but whose delight is in the law of the LORD, and who meditates on his law day and night. That person is like a tree planted by streams of water, which yields its fruit in season and whose leaf does not wither – whatever they do prospers.

Pause for Prayer

Think of your faith, for a moment, as a precious tree – planted by God's own hand. What must you do to care for it? How can you nourish and protect it in such a way that it grows?

Dear God, I thank you for this tree of faith. Help me to nurture it and tend it in such a way today that it brings a smile to your face, I pray. Amen.

Tale 16

A Rose to Remember

This particular day had been a long time coming. In November 2017, I had lost my wife and best friend to cancer. Fiona had been my steadfast and beloved companion throughout our thirty years of marriage. Together, we had raised three sons, who were all grown up now. Not long after I lost her, I started blogging my experience of the journey through the uncharted territory of grief in a series of posts entitled 'postcards from the land of grief'. They drew quite a following, formed the backbone of a radio broadcast which went around the world and helped to launch a national campaign on grief awareness at the Houses of Parliament. By early 2019, I had edited and compiled them into a book, *Postcards from the Land of Grief.* Various edits came and went, and by the end of July 2019, I held the first copy in my hand. When publication day came around, I had mixed feelings. On the one hand, I wished I had never been in a position to write such a book. On the other, I sincerely hoped that it might be of help to others who were travelling, alone, through the land of grief.

My question now was how to mark the day? There would be no formal book launch. Indeed, I am not sure I could have coped with it even if there had been. Instead, I made my way to what had become a familiar place of solace and inspiration – the local nursery. Rather like that one from childhood days, this is not a garden centre. There are no cookery books or novelty items. You cannot buy a lawnmower or a leaf blower there. This is a nursery, plain and simple. It sits on the edge of a forest and has rows and rows of outdoor flowerbeds and greenhouses. Early on in 'project garden', I had grown to love it. Often, I would go up there with a photo of a patch in my garden, show it to one of the helpful staff and ask what might grow there. My dog, Ginny, and I became frequent visitors. Often, she would sniff at the giant block of compost, more than 2 metres tall, in the potting shed as I waited to pay.

On this occasion, I was looking for help again. I explained that this was a special day. Today was publication day, and I wanted to plant something which I could look at and remember the day. Obviously, that was a little too vague even for the very patient staff, so I explained that I was thinking of a rose. Little did I know what I was asking. There were climbing roses and tea roses and hybrid roses and shrub roses. What did I want? In the end, we narrowed it down a little, and we walked along the rows together. Eventually I picked out a beautiful rose with peach petals tinged with pink, whose name was Evelyn May.

Arriving home, I planted it with great tenderness and admired its lovely flowers. When summer ended, I was cheered by the prospect that they would be back again the following year. Indeed, they were – in greater numbers and with greater vigour. This is a plant which looks like it belongs now. The blooms are a reminder that the seeds I planted in that book are flourishing too – unfurling their petals and releasing their scent in other lives.

I sometimes feel that if we could travel through the landscape of the Old Testament, we would find it littered with memorials of every kind. We would be forever tripping over a pile of stones here or a tree there, commemorating a person lost or a battle won. From this distance it all seems a little unnecessary. Except that it isn't. My years of ministry have taught me that we are all far too ready to forget the acts of God. The moment where a prayer is answered or a victory is won so easily evaporates when the next crisis comes along. Taking time to commemorate the acts of God in our lives is never wasted – and the effects can linger in helpful ways.

One year on from publication day, I looked out at my peach-coloured rose, saw the new buds unfurling – and thanked God that in the intervening year he had seen fit to bless the lives of others through that hard-written book.

Bible Reflection on Joshua 4:4–9

When Joshua and the people of Israel crossed the river Jordan, it was a miracle. The river was in flood season, and the waters would have been rushing by. I have always felt a little sorry for the priests, carrying the heavy Ark of the Covenant on their shoulders, who were told to step out first, trusting that the water would stop. They did and it did, and all crossed over safely. Imagine, though, if you had been one of the twelve asked to go back to the middle of the river and retrieve a rock as a memorial!

So Joshua called together the twelve men he had appointed from the Israelites, one from each tribe, and said to them, 'Go over before the ark of the LORD your God into the middle of the Jordan. Each of you is to take up a stone on his shoulder, according to the number of the tribes of the Israelites, to serve as a sign among you. In the future, when your children ask you, "What do these stones mean?" tell them that the flow of the Jordan was cut off before the ark of the covenant of the LORD. When it crossed the Jordan, the waters of the Jordan were cut off. These stones are to be a memorial to the people of Israel for ever.' So the Israelites did as Joshua commanded them. They took twelve stones from the middle of the Jordan, according to the number of the tribes of the Israelites, as the LORD had told Joshua; and they carried them over with them to their camp, where they put them down. Joshua set up the twelve stones that had been in the middle of the Jordan at the spot where the priests who carried the ark of the covenant had stood. And they are there to this day.

This was an act of memorial far more costly and dangerous than planting a rose!

Pause for Prayer

Why not take a moment to think back to the last time that a prayer was answered? It doesn't have to be anything huge or momentous – since having a prayer answered at all is quite a big deal! Once you have found that thing, dwell on it in your mind as you pray.

Lord, thank you for this answered prayer. Thank you that, with all the prayers in the whole world to listen to, this one did not go unnoticed. Whenever I grow forgetful about answered prayers, as I did with this one, remind me, I pray. Amen.

Tale 17

A Fruitful Responsibility

Since first breaking ground on that shabby bed in front of the shed, my view from the kitchen window had improved no end. As you know from the 'Ericaceous Error' chapter, the heathers weren't up to much, but my special rose was there. Not only that, but to the right were healthy, vigorous lavender and rosemary bushes, along with some flowering thyme and a new jasmine at the foot of my pergola. Maybe it was a sign of growing confidence that I was starting to see gaps where something new could go. Spaces vacated by rampant brambles would look so much better with some new occupant.

It was with this in mind that I headed to my beloved nursery. I had taken a compass reading to be sure that I knew what sort of aspect I was looking to fill. It was a position up against a south-facing fence with a good amount of sunshine and reasonable soil. I explained to the young assistant at the nursery that I was looking for something to occupy that space against the fence, and that I would like it to be something I could see easily from the kitchen window.

My heart sank a little when she led me towards the fruit trees. It sank even further when she led me towards the trained trees. These are trees that have been specially pruned to grow into a particular shape. The one in question was a 'Sunset' apple tree whose branches had been trained to grow in the elegant form of a fan. I started to shake my head, convinced that a novice gardener would be almost certain to kill such a serious plant. The assistant seemed amused, assuring me that if I planted it in a hole which was wide enough and watered it well throughout the summer, I should have no problems. Taking a deep breath, I made the purchase, and we slid it carefully into the back of the car, where it took up all the available space.

Once home, I dug a hole which was plenty big enough, added good-quality compost and tugged the hefty tree from its temporary home in the black plastic pot. Once in place, and level with the top of the hole, I back-filled, tamped the soil down, added mulch and watered it in. Feeling quite pleased with the purchase, I sent a photo to my skilful friend Henry, who complimented me on choosing such a young specimen. He explained that a younger tree would adjust to the trauma of being transplanted more readily than a big one. My pleasure was short-lived, though, when he reminded me that I would need to continue training the branches if the tree was to maintain its distinctive shape.

He was right. As well as all the watering which I was doing before, I now have to prune and train the tree too. Any branches or fruit which grow back from the main trunk towards the fence have to be removed. This way, the entire aspect of the tree is kept forwards, as it should be. As the main limbs of the tree have started to grow, I have had to extend beyond the canes supplied by the nursery with wire attached to my fence. To experienced gardeners reading this, that all sounds incredibly simple. To me, however, pruning and training are things done by other gardeners – the kind who *know* what they are doing!

Bible Reflection on John 15:1–8

On the night of his betrayal, Jesus took a walk with his disciples to the garden of Gethsemane. I have seen what remains of that garden for myself – and there are olive trees there which have been tended and nurtured for centuries. There may well have been vines too – trained and pruned to maximise their yield:

> I am the true vine, and my Father is the gardener. He cuts off every branch in me that bears no fruit, while every branch that does bear fruit he prunes so that it will be even more fruitful. You are already clean because of the word I have spoken to you. Remain in me, as I also remain in you. No branch can bear fruit by itself; it must remain in the vine. Neither can you bear fruit unless you remain in me. I am the vine; you are the branches. If you remain in me and I in you, you will bear much fruit; apart from me you can do nothing. If you do not remain in me, you are like a branch that is thrown away and withers; such branches are picked up, thrown into the fire and burned. If you remain in me and my words remain in you, ask whatever you wish, and it will be done for you. This is to my Father's glory, that you bear much fruit, showing yourselves to be my disciples.

If we are to adorn God's garden, there will be pruning. Thankfully, though, he has a better idea of what he is doing than I do.

Pause for Prayer

There is something which sounds very harsh about the whole idea of being pruned. Won't it hurt, just a little? Of course, sometimes it does. When God shapes our lives, some of the things which get taken away feel like a real loss at the time. What we can't see, though, is the overall shape he is creating.

> Dear God, today I have to talk to you about this whole idea of pruning. I know that I should trust you, and I know that you can see the whole shape of things. Because I can't, and because I'm afraid sometimes, I ask you to help me trust you today. Amen.

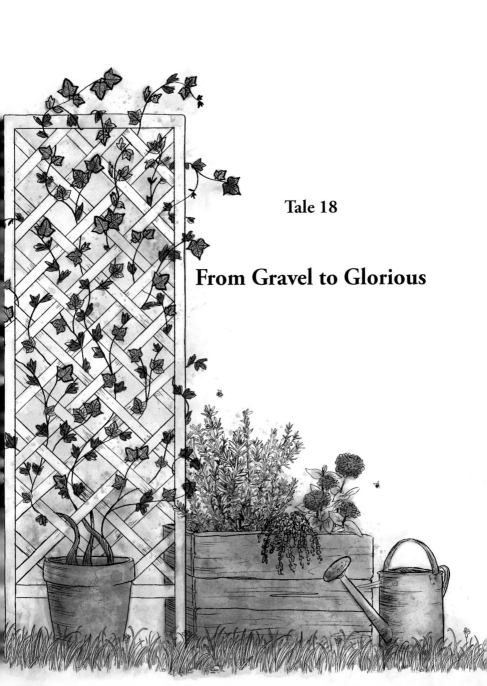

Tale 18

From Gravel to Glorious

I suppose it was inevitable that, as the back garden came gradually into shape, my thoughts would turn to the front. There wasn't much to it, in all honesty. Outside the front window was a paved driveway, with some gravel to the left-hand side. Under the window was an old laurel bush and a rather tired forsythia. Up against the front wall was a large and gangly Portuguese laurel tree. It was the gravel which really caught my eye. Nobody ever parked on it, and if their wheels rolled onto it by mistake, they would soon back away, with the sound of stones crunching in their tyre treads. As is often the case with gravel which has been there a while, it had long since lost its brightness. Not only that, but the weeds whose growth it was intended to inhibit seemed to delight in poking up through its surface with considerable vigour. Something had to be done.

I was hesitant to start, as the front garden was 'on display' and might attract the sort of queries which a 'proper' gardener could answer but which would leave me floundering. However, my mind was made up. The gravel had to go. I thought it would be a relatively easy job, but it was not. When I began, I had only a builder's bucket, a rake and a shovel to help me. Every evening, I was out there, filling buckets and carrying them through the garage to the back garden. Eventually, a friend offered me the use of a wheelbarrow, which sped the whole thing up no end. All the same, it was the best part of two weeks until I saw the soil which had lain under the gravel for more than twenty years. It was packed down as hard as concrete and immovably stuck to the weed-proof membrane which had been there all those years. At this point, a new tool came in, and I began to work to and fro across the hardened earth with a mattock.

By this stage, my mind was made up, and my new space was to be a meadow. I ordered the requisite amount of Berkshire meadow seed and had a month in hand until planting time. Every evening, I would go out and work back and forth across the soil with mattock and fork, turning it over and over. At the end of the month, I scattered my meadow seed, trod it in and set up sticks with lengths of Christmas tinsel to scare away the birds. After that I watched . . . and watched . . . and watched.

By my second spring in 'project garden', the bright green of the new planting was pushing up from the soil. Early summer came, and the different grasses were at waist height. Some were pure green, some were red fescue with a tint of deep red at the edges. In amongst them were yellow rattle and, here and there, the impossible powder-blue flash of a cornflower. Time and again I have sat at my desk, mesmerised as the tall grasses bob and dance in the breeze. How could *this* have been *that*?

Of course, I should not really have been surprised. My Christian faith has been with me since the age of 16, and I know deep down that God is in the business of transformation. If he can make the 'deserts rejoice' and 'flowers bloom in the wilderness' (see Isa. 35:1), then why was my little patch of gravel such a surprise?

Bible Reflection on Ephesians 3:20,21

Sometimes, believing in God can be a tough ask. Christians living in the ancient city of Ephesus were in a place so rife with magic and curses that an 'Ephesian letter' was a nickname for a magic spell. The city's skyline was dominated by the 25,000-seater temple to the pagan goddess Diana. This was not a good or easy place to be a Christian. That said, look how Paul concludes his prayer for them:

> Now to him who is able to do immeasurably more than all we ask or imagine, according to his power that is at work within us, to him be glory in the church and in Christ Jesus throughout all generations, for ever and ever! Amen.

For God to do more than we can ask or imagine is, quite literally, beyond our imagination. Maybe we can't look at the gravel and see the meadow, but he can.

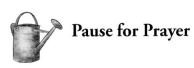

Pause for Prayer

Take a look across your life right now, as I look out across my little meadow. Do you see something that you want to change, but it just feels impossible? Can you see only the tired gravel and the persistent weeds? Now is the time to ask God for the courage to do something new.

Dear God, you know how easily defeated I feel. When I look out at this bit of my life right now, all I can see is the weeds. Help me to believe that something new and lovely could grow in their place. Help me to do something about it, I pray. Amen.

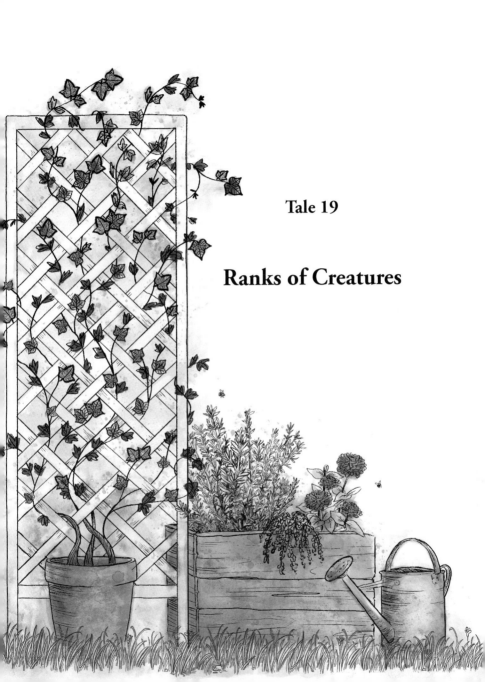

Tale 19

Ranks of Creatures

There's an old hymn 'At the Name of Jesus', written by Caroline Maria Noel in 1870. It contains the following line: 'Through all ranks of creatures, to the central height'.

I have always found it to be a slightly odd description, as I never felt that the creatures were ranked. Surely *all* are God's creatures – from the smallest flea to the most enormous whale? Of course, that is not entirely true. Human beings are naturally drawn to creatures which seem human in their actions or expressions. All the same, I have always felt as if we ought to see them all in the same way.

In truth, I know it is not so. Take the birds which visit my garden, for instance. There are pigeons, blackbirds, robins, various members of the tit family, a nuthatch, a lesser-spotted woodpecker and, on one memorable occasion, even a hen pheasant. The latter came for several days, and every time she looked bewildered as if she had landed here by accident. She would strut around the garden, in that distinctive way that pheasants have, as though afraid of breaking something by putting her feet down too firmly. Mind you, she would tease the dog mercilessly, often leaving it until she was all but snapping at her tail feathers before taking flight.

Do you realise how much space I have taken up there talking about just one bird? Because I regarded her as slightly more exotic, the camera would come out on almost every visit. The same goes for the woodpecker, even now. With his smart black and white plumage and his cardinal's cap of scarlet, I simply can't resist trying to capture his photograph.

Despite the faithful robin who turns up every time I turn any piece of soil in the garden, it is the woodpecker which has the camera clicking. It is all a bit fickle really.

That aside, gardening has taught me to recognise the value of some far less exotic creatures. My heart swells with joy every time I see the bees buzzing around anything that I have planted. Their buzz is a happy sound – the sound of summer and the sound of abundance. Not only that, but every time I am digging, or turning over the soil, I 'harvest' worms with something akin to reverence, that I might accommodate them in the luxury penthouse of my compost heap. I know that they will be well-fed there, and I know that my plants will benefit from it. Even the least beautiful creature has a place in God's order of things.

Bible Reflection on James 2:1–8

Most of us love to think that we are the kind of people who would never discriminate. All the same, we find ourselves doing it unconsciously – giving more deference and respect to some than others. This is not a new problem by any means. James writes here when the church was still quite new:

> My brothers and sisters, believers in our glorious Lord Jesus Christ must not show favouritism. Suppose a man comes into your meeting wearing a gold ring and fine clothes, and a poor man in filthy old clothes also comes in. If you show special attention to the man wearing fine clothes and say, 'Here's a good seat for you,' but say to the poor man, 'You stand there' or 'Sit on the floor by my feet,' have you not discriminated among yourselves and become judges with evil thoughts? Listen, my dear brothers and sisters: has not God chosen those who are poor in the eyes of the world to be rich in faith and to inherit the kingdom he promised those who love him? But you have dishonoured the poor. Is it not the rich who are exploiting you? Are they not the ones who are dragging you into court? Are they not the ones who are blaspheming the noble name of him to whom you belong? If you really keep the royal law found in Scripture, 'Love your neighbour as yourself,' you are doing right.

I am hoping that my new appreciation of those beasts further down the 'rank of creatures' might remind me not to look down at any people either.

Pause for Prayer

Take a moment to look out across the 'landscape' of the people known to you. Be really honest, and ask yourself if you ever treat some of them as being more important than others. If the answer is 'yes', then even seeing it is a step towards putting it right.

Dear God, I truly am sorry for those moments when I have treated some people as more important than others. Now that I have noticed it, will you help me to do something about it, I pray? Amen.

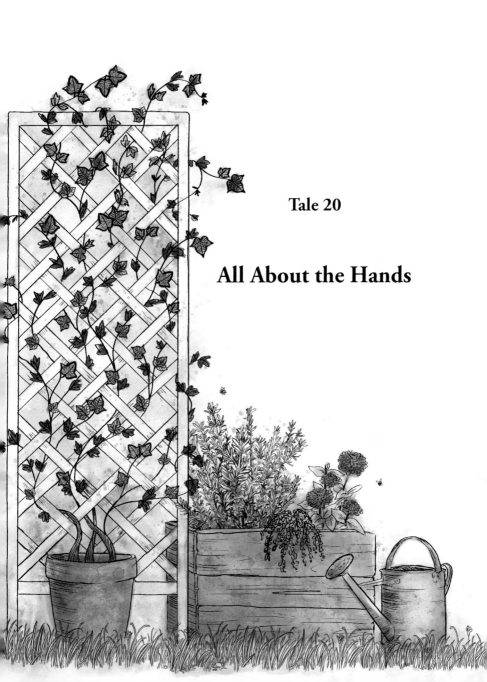

Tale 20

All About the Hands

I'm not proud of it, but nonetheless, it is true. I love gadgets. I love the thrill of sliding them out of the packaging and firing them up. I love their lights and switches and displays and noises. Given this, the world of gardening should have opened up all sorts of possibilities for me – there are power tools of every description out there for the asking. I could have cut branches, trimmed bushes, blown leaves and more, all at the flick of a switch.

However, when the first autumn in my new-found garden came, a curious thing happened. Every day, the leaves were coming down from the trees surrounding the garden by their hundreds. They would blow and scud about in the wind or gather in drifts like snow. Two or three times, I looked at leaf blowers and leaf vacuums of different descriptions. I never bought one, though. The strange thing is that I liked raking the leaves up. I enjoyed the rhythmic, soothing motion of the rake clattering across the grass and pulling them all together. If I went out every day, it was not a long task, but it connected me with my garden realm. I looked forward to that visit out there each day, cold wind pinching at my cheeks or autumn damp settling on my hair. Not only that, but I braved the DIY demons and made an enclosure in which to store all the leaves whilst they broke down. As autumn rolled by, so the leaves got wet and dry, dry and wet – turning eventually into leaf mould. Early the next spring, I would mulch the garden beds with it, and the whole cycle would begin again.

It was maybe this experience which made me cut my meadow by hand the following summer too. It had given me such pleasure since those early days in the spring when the first shoots had pushed up and up.

In the height of summer, it had been like a moving tapestry, some stems almost a metre high, and dotted here and there with baby-blue cornflowers. I knew, though, that to maintain its vigour, it would need to be cut down to less than 15 centimetres at the end of the summer. Would the man who had raked the leaves by hand turn a strimmer on his beloved meadow? It turned out that he would not. Instead, I bought a small Japanese sickle and worked my way across the meadow with kneeling mat and sickle. The hiss of the blade through the grass stems was deeply satisfying, and there was a new magnificence about those tall stems as they lay flat, drying in the sun. The whole process with this meadow, from gravel-lifting, to breaking up with a mattock, to digging and planting and now to harvesting, had been by hand – and it felt so good.

I love the fact that God made human beings by hand. The rest of creation springs into being at the mere sound of his voice, but for human beings he rolls up his sleeves and gets his hands dirty. At some point near the dawn of creation, damp clay sat in the very palm of God, picking up the whorls of his fingertips as he shaped it. That clay became man.

Bible Reflection on Jeremiah 18:1–6

Being a prophet was a tough ask, whichever way you looked at it. On the one hand, you were privy to the often-troubling insights of God. On the other, you were expected to pass them on – often to an audience less than willing to hear them. In such a situation, it was important that the prophet should not only hear but feel and understand the message of God. On the brink of one of his toughest and least popular assignments, Jeremiah was sent on a 'field trip' by God:

> This is the word that came to Jeremiah from the LORD: 'Go down to the potter's house, and there I will give you my message.' So I went down to the potter's house, and I saw him working at the wheel. But the pot he was shaping from the clay was marred in his hands; so the potter formed it into another pot, shaping it as seemed best to him. Then the word of the LORD came to me. He said, 'Can I not do with you, Israel, as this potter does?' declares the LORD. 'Like clay in the hand of the potter, so are you in my hand, Israel.

Jeremiah had to see the potter at his work, hear the wheel turning and watch the wet clay ooze through his fingers before he could really understand what God was saying. In this instance, dirty hands made for a clear mind.

Pause for Prayer

Is there some area of your life where you have been hesitant to get your hands dirty? It might be a messy relationship, or even an avenue of service which scares you. Why not speak, today, to the God with dirty hands?

Dear God, you know my fears even better than I know them myself. You know that I am hesitant to 'plunge in' on this, in case things get messy. Help me, today, to take a deep breath and take your hand. Amen.

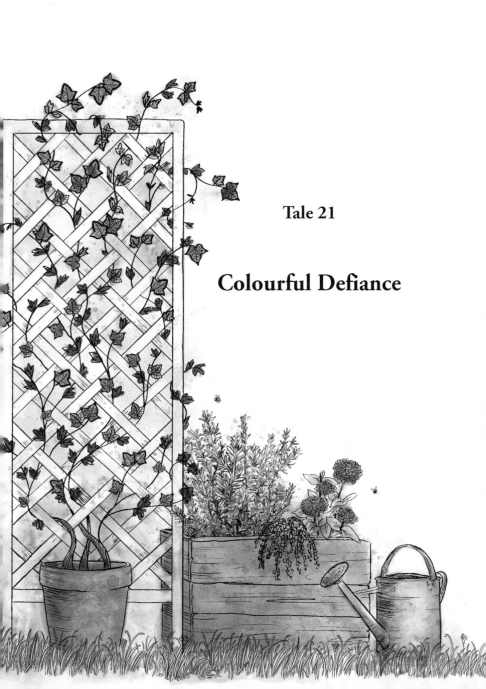

Tale 21

Colourful Defiance

One of the great advantages of being new to gardening is that nobody minds your obvious ignorance! When I was removing the gravel from my front garden to make way for my meadow, I came across a peculiar thing. It was about the size and shape of a small sweet potato and a dark chestnut-brown colour. There seemed to be roots and tendrils coming out in all directions, and it was not immediately apparent which way was up! As I often did at the time, I posted a picture on social media and asked for help. Whilst some made quirky suggestions that it might have come from outer space, others were more helpful. Overall, people concluded that it was a rhizome, or underground plant stem, from which roots would develop at the right time. Most people thought it was probably a cyclamen.

Knowing them to be a woodland flower, I carried my ugly, knobbly find through to the back garden and planted it beneath the trunk of a large buddleia tree. As the project to clear the front garden of gravel proceeded through the early summer, I found more and more of them. With each one, I did the same. I carefully dug around it so as not to damage it. I then carried it through to its new home, dug a hole, added some compost and refilled the hole. To be honest, I did so with more hope than anticipation. How could these ugly things, which I may well have damaged in lifting them, survive, let alone flourish?

When winter came, I was to find myself wonderfully proven wrong. As the days got shorter and darker and most of the other plants died back, a little revolution was happening at the foot of my buddleia tree. Red, pink and white splashes of colour were emerging from the soil where I had planted those ugly, misshapen rhizomes. My cyclamen were coming good. All through the darkest days of winter, with dead leaves round about and frost laced across their petals, these plucky little plants kept up a wonderful display.

The gravel and the weed-proof membrane under which they had lain had been there for at least twenty years, so these plants were grasping their second chance with a vengeance. On the coldest days of winter, when even the keenest gardener would think twice about venturing out, the sight of their defiant brightness in the shadows would lift my spirits.

Bible Reflection on Isaiah 45:1–3 (NKJV)

The prophet Isaiah was a man with a bright message in dark times. Exile had ruined the people's sense of themselves, their glorious history was a distant memory and faith was hard to find. In the midst of all this, though, God had a plan. Cyrus, a Babylonian king, would be God's key to unlock the door and let the people go:

> Thus, says the LORD to His anointed,
> To Cyrus, whose right hand I have held –
> To subdue nations before him
> And loose the armor of kings,
> To open before him the double doors,
> So that the gates will not be shut:
> 'I will go before you
> And make the crooked places straight;
> I will break in pieces the gates of bronze
> And cut the bars of iron.
> I will give you the treasures of darkness
> And hidden riches of secret places,
> That you may know that I, the LORD,
> Who call you by your name,
> Am the God of Israel.'

Those verses have been a bright light to me in some of the darkest days of my life. It is for this reason that I have chosen a translation reading *'treasures of darkness'*. These treasures, like my bright cyclamen on a dark winter's afternoon, have brought both light and joy.

Pause for Prayer

Do you have hopes or dreams buried deep down, like those rhizomes buried beneath my gravel? Do you fear that they will never see the light of day, or that they might not survive if they did? Today is a good day to take them out in the private space of prayer and tell God all about them.

Dear God, these dreams look like battered, fragile things in the cold light of day. Could it be that I could make something of them yet? Help me to hear you, and trust you with them, I pray. Amen.

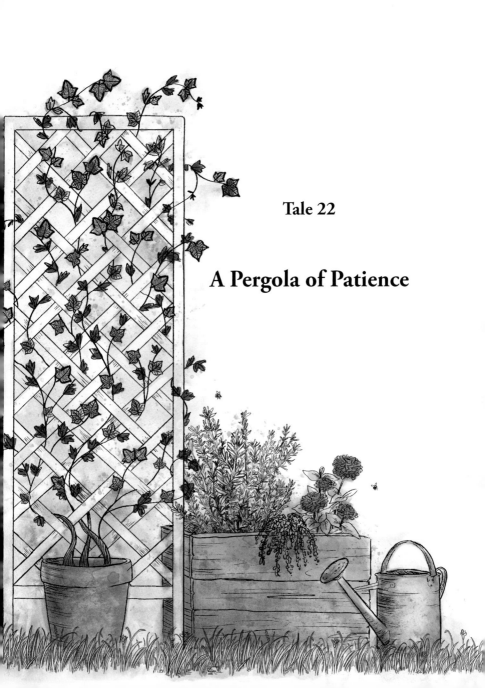

Tale 22

A Pergola of Patience

At the bottom of the garden was an old pergola. It had been built by a previous occupant of the house and steadily fallen into disrepair. Once upon a time, it had played host to the 'dreaded bench' of a previous tale. It didn't take much to bring it to life, though. I removed the old bench, weeded between the paving cracks and scrubbed them clean. At the front of the paving was a strip of old gravel, long since lost to the weeds. I dug both weeds and gravel out and replaced them all with a mixture of red and white gypsum. The bright white stones reflected the sun up into this pleasant corner. A friend and I spent an afternoon working above our heads to fix some mesh with artificial ivy leaves onto the roof of the pergola, and my neglected corner became a haven of dappled shade. Occasionally, I sit down there to look at the garden from a different angle, and it has been known to double as a studio for my BBC Radio 4 recordings too. All these changes have been physically demanding but quick. Not all garden changes are so.

One of the changes which had come over *me* was that I was no longer embarrassed by the garden. No longer did I wince as people turned to look out of the back windows. In fact, I often invited them to come and take a look. On one such occasion, I made a tour of the garden with a friend, a skilled and thoughtful gardener herself. She looked at my pergola, rested a hand on the left pillar and said, 'You need a jasmine on there – buy the biggest you can afford.' The next week, I followed her advice and selected a lovely pink summer jasmine. By the next summer, I thought, it would be climbing up and across my shady nook and releasing its heady perfume. For the first few months, it did indeed grow, spreading feathery lime-green leaves as it went. Then it stopped.

The stems were still growing, but the leaves were brittle and dull. Every wiser gardening head assured me that this was no more than a setback and that, by the following summer, all would be well. They were right, and all was indeed well – but I think my patience had to grow a little with those light green leaves and the tiny, tiny pink buds.

The apostle Peter once wrote to his friends that 'with the Lord a day is like a thousand years, and a thousand years are like a day' (2 Pet. 3:8). In my heart, I know it to be true – but it might take me another 1,000 years to learn it!

Bible Reflection on Luke 2:25–32

There are many people in the pages of the Bible whom I would like to meet, and there is an old man called Simeon who is fairly high up the list. We don't know his age, but we do know that he had been waiting and waiting for his moment. If he could just hold on, he had been told, he would see something truly miraculous:

> Now there was a man in Jerusalem called Simeon, who was right-eous and devout. He was waiting for the consolation of Israel, and the Holy Spirit was on him. It had been revealed to him by the Holy Spirit that he would not die before he had seen the Lord's Messiah. Moved by the Spirit, he went into the temple courts. When the parents brought in the child Jesus to do for him what the custom of the Law required, Simeon took him in his arms and praised God, saying:

> 'Sovereign Lord, as you have promised, you may now dismiss your servant in peace. For my eyes have seen your salvation, which you have prepared in the sight of all nations: a light for revelation to the Gentiles, and the glory of your people Israel.'

I think Simeon could teach me a lot about patience. That said, by the time I get to meet him, I suppose I shan't need it any more.

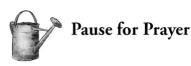

Pause for Prayer

Is there some area of your life right now where you feel that God is just taking far too long to sort things out? It might be a plea for guidance or an earnest prayer for someone you love. Why hasn't he answered yet? This would be a good moment to tell him about it, maybe even by writing it down on a piece of paper which no one else ever needs to see.

Dear God, you know that I have been waiting and waiting to see some change in this. I have tried to be patient, but sometimes my patience gets stretched like an elastic band, and I worry that it will snap. If today is not the day that this thing is going to change, then could you please reassure me, at least, that you have not forgotten my pleas? I thank you for this and for your patience with me. Amen.

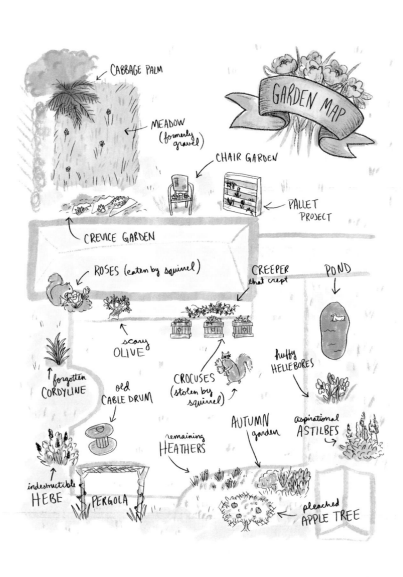

CABBAGE PALM

GARDEN MAP

MEADOW (formerly gravel)

CHAIR GARDEN

PALLET PROJECT

CREVICE GARDEN

ROSES (eaten by squirrel)

CREEPER that crept

POND

scary OLIVE

↑ forgotten CORDYLINE

old CABLE DRUM

CROCUSES (stolen by squirrel)

huffy HELLEBORES

remaining HEATHERS

AUTUMN garden

aspirational ASTILBES

indestructible HEBE

PERGOLA

pleached APPLE TREE

Tale 23

Planting Now for Then

About two years before 'project garden' began, I had rediscovered an old hobby. With the help of a friend in the church, I had constructed a baseboard in the loft on which a model railway layout was unfolding. At the time, it was something on which I could work whilst being just a few steps away from my wife, resting in bed, in case she needed me. 'Little Dale', as it became known, had all sorts. There was a huge chalky hill, with the obligatory tunnel, and an old mine shaft. There was a canal, complete with a basin for the narrow boats. There was a small goods yard, a viaduct and a shopping street. Other features included a shunting yard, a replica of a local castle and a landscape dotted with long barrows. It all sounds very elaborate, and I suppose in some ways it was. However, it was also very do-able. With the right degree of concentration, I could erect a forest, demolish a hill or create a townscape in an afternoon. Not so with gardening, I fear.

Of course, at first, I bought things for instant impact. I bought heathers and geraniums that were flowering, which instantly brought my containers to life. Then I started to seek advice from those who knew, far better idea than I, what they were doing. The staff in my local nursery were patience itself and listened with interest to my vague descriptions of a bed which 'looks a bit like this' and 'faces that sort of way', and has a 'a big shrub with waxy green leaves growing at the back'. Each time, they would give me their recommendations, and each time I would come home with some new plant to fill up my newly emptied beds. Except, of course, they didn't. If I look out of the window just now, I can see two choisyas, one with yellow leaves and one with green. They are about 4 centimetres bigger than they were last year, and no more. I now know, from other people's gardens, that in four or six years' time they will look as if they were always there – but not yet.

Gradually, the insight has started to rub off. At the bottom of the garden is the bed where this all began, next to the shed. For several months I have been planting things there, which look dull and uninteresting right now. They will need some time to get established, but their time will come. When next autumn arrives with all its golden colours, and in the winter after that, when so many things die back, they will come into their own. They have been planted for their bright red bark and their rich autumnal foliage, not their flowers. In short, they are planted *now* for *then*.

After more than thirty years of ministry, and nineteen of those in the same place, I am starting to learn the value of planting *now* for *then*. The children's talks of *today* can be the teenage truths of *tomorrow*. The wedding sermon *now* can be the parenting lifeline *then*. Sometimes we 'sow in tears' now, as the psalmist says, hoping to 'reap in joy' then (see Ps. 126:5, NKJV).

Bible Reflection on Matthew 6:19–21

The phrase 'treasures in heaven' has become so well known in its own right that few would necessarily know that it springs from the Bible. It is to be found in the Sermon on the Mount, Jesus' *teach-in* at the heart of Matthew's gospel. The sermon consists of three chapters of consolidated teaching on the nature of the kingdom of God. It is an extended recalibration of the soul's compass to the values of that kingdom. In these verses, Jesus reminds his listeners to think now of then:

> Do not store up for yourselves treasures on earth, where moths and vermin destroy, and where thieves break in and steal. But store up for yourselves treasures in heaven, where moths and vermin do not destroy, and where thieves do not break in and steal. For where your treasure is, there your heart will be also.

A lesson we all have to learn as followers of Jesus is that the things we prepare now will bloom then – a bit like my optimistic choisyas.

Pause for Prayer

Is there some area of life or service where you feel you have been investing heavily, to no avail? Perhaps you have been praying for one particular person or explaining your faith to them, all with no discernible result? Maybe this is a slow-growing plant that God's planting *now* for *then*? Today is a good day to trust him with it afresh.

> Dear God, you know that I have been trying and trying to make things happen in this situation. Today, I'm not going to stop trying, but I will do my best to stop worrying. Today, I shall leave the worrying to you. Amen.

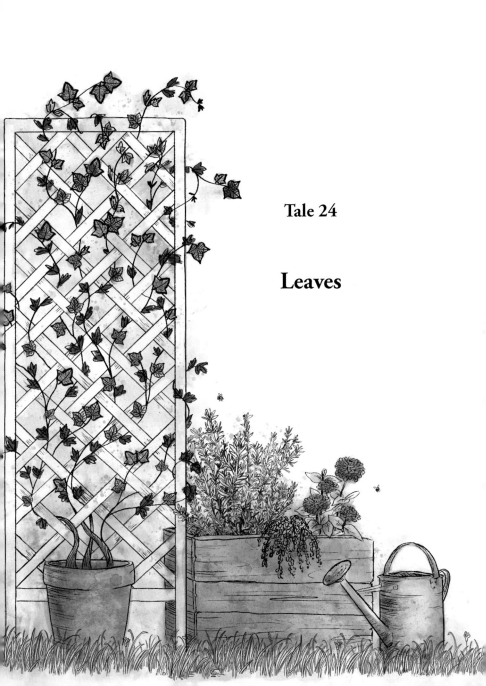

Tale 24

Leaves

Back on that heady summer day when Henry rode to my rescue and helped with my planting, he had done something else too. To the right of the garden was a very vigorous shrub. Although it was attractive, it was hogging the light and making it impossible to grow anything else within its shadow. I had started, very tentatively, to cut it back. I snipped a bit here and a bit there, but it was not enough to really make a difference. He reached deep into the branches, pointed out the scars of where it had been cut back years before and encouraged me to go further. 'Cut it back to where you want it to be,' he said, 'and then keep it there.'

Once he had gone, I continued on into the evening doing just that. The further I went, the bigger the tools became. In the end, I was using a saw to cut off the bigger branches. By the time I was done, the pile of debris behind me was (not surprisingly) as big as the shrub had been. The smaller bits were snipped up and put in to the garden rubbish bin – but what to do with the serious, thick, branches? At that point, that old adage of my father's that 'it will come in handy' kicked in – and I stored four or five of them down the side of the shed.

When the autumn of that first year came, sweeping up the leaves became a daily task. As you now know, it was one which I relished. However, there was the question about where to put the leaves once I had collected them. Various gardening experts said that they should be kept and turned into leaf mould for mulch the following year. That was all very well, but most of the articles about doing so contained the intimidating word 'make'. I needed to 'make' a chicken wire enclosure for the leaves, so that they could be stored in such a way as to let the air circulate. At this point, four of my kept branches came out from the side of the shed. I picked the straightest ones, inexpertly hacked at the ends to make a point, fixed the chicken wire into them and hammered the whole lot into the ground as a rough 'leaf enclosure'. The first time I tipped a bucket or two of leaves in, I was astonished to see that the whole thing did not fall over. Not only that, but it worked. By the next spring, I had leaves which had broken down enough to mix with compost and mulch the awakening garden. Who would have thought that a DIY scheme could go right?

As a pastor, I have seen again and again that people are afraid to go beyond their prior experience for fear of 'getting it wrong'. It might be that things have fallen out awkwardly before, or simply that they fear they might. Full of potential to bless through their untested gifts, the church remains poorer as long as those with giftings are hidden. To be fair, it doesn't always go completely right the first time. My leaf enclosure wobbled a bit until there were enough leaves inside to prop it up completely. In the end it did the job, though – which I would never have known unless I tried.

Bible Reflection on Judges 6:11–16

Things were bad in Israel at the time of Gideon. Cross-border raids from aggressive neighbours were commonplace. Gideon himself was so afraid that he was threshing wheat inside the confined space of a wine-press, rather than out in the open air. When an angel of God appears and greets him as a 'mighty warrior', it is not altogether surprising that he is taken aback:

> The angel of the LORD came and sat down under the oak in Ophrah that belonged to Joash the Abiezrite, where his son Gideon was threshing wheat in a winepress to keep it from the Midianites. When the angel of the LORD appeared to Gideon, he said, 'The LORD is with you, mighty warrior.' 'Pardon me, my lord,' Gideon replied, 'but if the LORD is with us, why has all this happened to us? Where are all his wonders that our ancestors told us about when they said, "Did not the LORD bring us up out of Egypt?" But now the LORD has abandoned us and given us into the hand of Midian.' The LORD turned to him and said, 'Go in the strength you have and save Israel out of Midian's hand. Am I not sending you?' 'Pardon me, my lord,' Gideon replied, 'but how can I save Israel? My clan is the weakest in Manasseh, and I am the least in my family.' The LORD answered, 'I will be with you, and you will strike down all the Midianites, leaving none alive.'

The angel was as good as his word, and Gideon did indeed win a great victory. All the same, I would love to have been a fly on the wall to see his look of astonishment when the angel came. To hear, and then see, that you can do more than you ever thought possible is the very best kind of surprise.

 **Pause for Prayer**

Have you been asked, or challenged, to do something for God and it all seems a bit much? Know that your hesitation is no surprise at all to God. I suspect the angel had a little bit of a wry grin on his face when he addressed Gideon as a 'mighty warrior'! Why not tell God honestly about those fears – and see where things go from there?

Dear God, sometimes I am so caught up with past mistakes that I can't see future possibilities. Today, show me something new and unexpected that I can do for you, I pray. Amen.

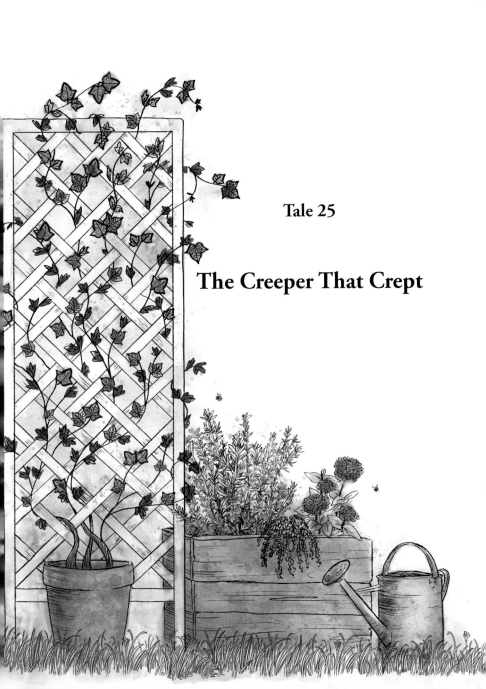

Tale 25

The Creeper That Crept

I was reaching the end of my first calendar year of gardening. The leaves had all been carefully swept up and stored in their new enclosure; the last growth of summer had all died away. One or two cyclamen were coming up as defiant splashes of red and pink – but apart from that, the garden was getting ready to settle in under the duvet for winter. All with one exception, that is.

The church house, or manse, in which I live has a substantial area of decking at the back. The years had taken their toll, and the timbers were starting to sway a bit whenever anybody walked across them. During autumn of the first year, two workmen worked tirelessly in wind, rain and sun to get a new one built. As their task was nearing its end, they offered to create some planters from the spare timber to stand against the front wall of the decking. I gladly accepted and was pleased when I later saw three solid, cube-shaped planters waiting for planting.

As the workmen were gone for the weekend, I followed their advice on the planters. I bought a big sheet of damp-proof lining and set about creating a deep 'hammock' inside each one. The bottom of each hammock was duly perforated, before adding gravel, soil and potting compost. A trip to my favourite garden centre brought enough heucheras and ivies to fill each planter to left and right. The heucheras would grow upwards and outwards with their soft, autumnal colours, and the ivies would cascade pleasingly over the edge. That left the central planter.

This called for a trip to a nursery rather than a garden centre. I described the location that I had in mind and explained I would like a Virginia creeper to climb up and across the front of the decking. There used to be one in the car park of my local library, and I had fallen in love with the rich red of its leaves. The plantsman nodded sagely and then disappeared off to find me a suitable plant. When he returned, he had a large black pot with what could charitably be described as a 'twig' in the middle. It was one of the most scrawny and pathetic plants I had ever seen. However, he assured me that it had 'lovely roots' and would do well.

For a couple of months, it just sat there, with not the slightest sign of life. The following January, the tiniest of red buds appeared here and there along its twiggy branches. More and more appeared, and things started to happen. When the summer of the second year arrived, the creeper was almost 2 metres long, with a cascade of lush green leaves which spread by the day. When the time comes, all those leaves should turn a gorgeous shade of red. How right that plantsman was to see its hidden potential.

Every once in a while, I look in the mirror and wonder why ever God would pick a person like me to do a job like this. Can't he see my faults? Of course, the answer is that he can. However, he also sees beyond them to the potential – like my plantsman with the 'lovely roots'.

Bible Reflection on Philippians 1:3–6

It must have been quite a pressure living in a city whose name meant 'brotherly love'. What a pressure on the Christians in the city of Philippi, especially, to act differently. Paul, however, seems to have great plans for them:

> I thank my God every time I remember you. In all my prayers for all of you, I always pray with joy because of your partnership in the gospel from the first day until now, being confident of this, that he who began a good work in you will carry it on to completion until the day of Christ Jesus.

Like the plantsman, he could see that they would grow and flourish one day.

Pause for Prayer

I am convinced my creeper will continue beautifully; I really am. That conviction is strong, despite my complete ignorance of what would make it grow or why it has 'lovely roots'. Every time I brush my fingertips through its lush green foliage, my faith in its future grows.

Today would be a good day to tell God about a plan or a dream of yours which fills you with hope. It doesn't have to be anything enormous, just something special. Tell him about it now, and then ask for faith and patience as you wait for it to be.

Dear God, I'm almost too shy to tell you about this dream of mine. It seems too big and too improbable, but I know you won't laugh. As I lay it at your feet now, stir up my faith that you hold all good things in your hands. Amen.

Tale 26

The Joy of Tidying

There is at least one person who will throw back her head and laugh when she reads the title of this chapter. That person is my mum. As a little boy, my failure to embrace any kind of tidying gene was legendary. Generally, I would wait until the tide of half-read books, half-built models and toys was lapping around the foot of the bed before I yielded to entreaties to tidy it up. Eventually, I would do so, and then the whole cycle would start all over again.

As my first gardening year was drawing to a close, I found that there was a great joy in tidying things away as autumn turned to winter. To fold up the chairs and pack up the sunshade where I had sat on those long summer evenings brought a sort of melancholy with it, to be sure. However, there was something else. There was also a sense of anticipation. To pack away these things meant that autumn was gone and her sharper cousin, winter, was coming, of course. After them, though, would come the energy of spring and the glories of summer. Even something as mundane as packing away the garden furniture served as a reminder of the rhythms of life.

It was not just the furniture which had to be packed away, either. There were the plants too. Into my cold frame went an old copper fish kettle, planted up with dwarf alpine plants. Beside that went a bulbous cream planter which had spent spring and summer by my front door, soaking up the heat and turning it into fleshy rosettes of pink leaves on my houseleeks. Now it would need protecting until warmer, drier days came again. With no greenhouse, I had to do my best for other plants in containers. My climbing rose, my beautiful pink cordyline and one or two others were all moved up close to the house wall and grouped together, like friends huddling to ride out the storm. The most delicate ones had their pots enclosed in thick bubble wrap and parcel tape. A few months later, the joy at ripping that packaging off when spring was in the air would be palpable.

Meanwhile, plants in the garden were making their own preparations. Tall plants whose seed heads were now empty were finally giving up and dying back, whilst those which had lain dormant were coming into their own. Cyclamen, whose ugly, alien rhizomes lay hidden under the soil, were now thrusting through the cold earth and showing their pink and white buds. When winter came, they would be laced with frost, as if a child had scattered them with glitter.

These rhythms had been there all along, of course. Long ago, when the flood waters had started to recede around Noah's ark, God had said:

> As long as the earth endures, seedtime and harvest, cold and heat, summer and winter, day and night will never cease.
>
> *Genesis 8:22*

There was nothing new about all this. What was new was that I was starting to appreciate it.

Bible Reflection on Ecclesiastes 3:1–11

Sometimes wisdom consists not of knowing lots of facts but of understanding the deeper truths beneath them. King Solomon was legendary for his wisdom, but some of it comprised a simple coming to terms with the way things are:

> There is a time for everything, and a season for every activity under the heavens: a time to be born and a time to die, a time to plant and a time to uproot, a time to kill and a time to heal, a time to tear down and a time to build, a time to weep and a time to laugh, a time to mourn and a time to dance, a time to scatter stones and a time to gather them, a time to embrace and a time to refrain from embracing, a time to search and a time to give up, a time to keep and a time to throw away, a time to tear and a time to mend, a time to be silent and a time to speak, a time to love and a time to hate, a time for war and a time for peace. What do workers gain from their toil? I have seen the burden God has laid on the human race. He has made everything beautiful in its time. He has also set eternity in the human heart; yet no one can fathom what God has done from beginning to end.

Centuries after those words were written, a man folding up his deckchair under the gathering clouds of autumn rain would begin to understand what they meant.

Pause for Prayer

Deep down in each one of us, like the rhizomes of my cyclamen buried out of sight, there needs to be a trust that all things run to God's timetable. It may be very different to our own, of course – but we need to trust that it is there all the same. The failure to do so leads to us fighting the seasons of the soul – like a spring flower coming up in winter and getting beaten back by the cold weather.

Dear God, today I ask that you would help me to take a deep breath and to trust that all things work to your plan. If I can't see it, or even really believe that it is there, then today I ask you to give me just a little bit more faith. Amen.

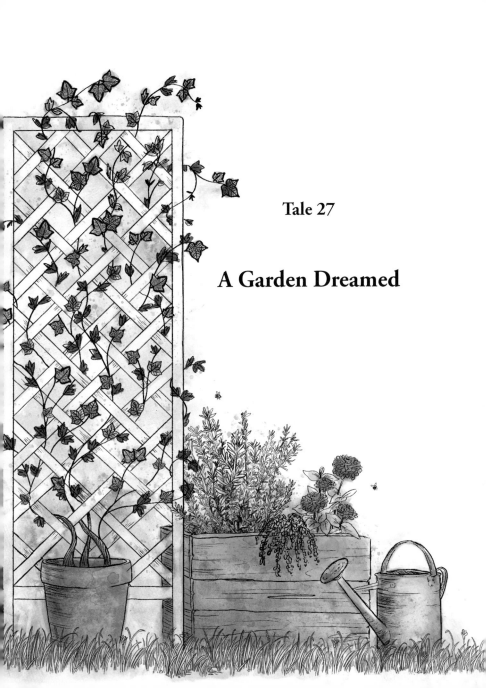

Tale 27

A Garden Dreamed

I have a dream. It is not a particularly noble or earth-shattering one, but it is a dream nonetheless. In that dream, someone comes to visit me, and we land up in the kitchen as I make a tea or coffee. Catching sight of the garden out of the window, they ask if they can see it whilst the kettle boils, and I am happy to oblige. As we walk to the edge of the decking, there is an audible gasp at the sight which greets them.

To their right is a flowerbed anchored at one corner by the tall, architectural structure of a phormium, flanked to right and left by the healthy green leaves of a butcher's broom and a New Zealand tea tree. Moving down that bed, beneath the mock orange (Philadelphus), three glorious choisyas stand about a metre tall, well-rounded and speckled with tiny white flowers. At their feet is a small carpet of mauve storksbill, the flowers nibbling at the edge of the lawn. Next come the grasses – many shades and heights, some bobbing in the breeze. Beyond that is a cottage garden with rounded and gorgeous hebes growing beneath a fragrant jasmine and accompanied by a riot of this year's colourful garden annuals. Their eye moves across the herb bed and the autumn border, with its dogwoods, ninebark and pleached apple tree. Underneath the trees on the other side is a woodland garden with a carpet of tiarella and the tall spikes of pink and white astilbes lighting up the dappled shade. Beyond that comes the pond, flanked by lush ferns and finally the callicarpas with their lustrous purple berries and the dahlias to take their breath away. The whole thing is centred round an emerald lawn of such perfection that they would hesitate to walk on it.

This particular garden exists only in my dreams, at least for now. The lawn is a racetrack for my beloved lurcher and bears the scars. My choisyas are struggling to make 50 centimetres or so just now, and the storksbills are only getting started. The hebes are barely 30 centimetres high and the cottage garden struggles every year to rise above artful mess to colourful mess. The astilbes can't decide whether they like my woodland patch, and only one of my dahlias remains. It doesn't hurt to dream, though.

In truth, this is slightly more than a dream. At least, it is a dream lodged under my fingernails and forming callouses on my hands. It is a dream buried with the thorn in my finger and running up the aching muscles of my back. It is a dream for which I am prepared to work and for which I love to plan. In short, it is a dream not unlike God's view of the church – a place of light and hope and kingdom reflections wherever you look. That, at least, is the way it will be . . .

Bible Reflection on Ephesians 5:25–27

If I were Paul, I think I might just have given up on the churches long before prison took me away from them. They were, by turns, anxious, fretful, fractious and downright combative. Despite all of that, he still appears to believe the best of them. Writing to Christians in the oppressively pagan city of Ephesus, he describes a church such as he had never yet seen:

> Husbands, love your wives, just as Christ loved the church and gave himself up for her to make her holy, cleansing her by the washing with water through the word, and to present her to himself as a radiant church, without stain or wrinkle or any other blemish, but holy and blameless.

I think it is fair to say that such a church did not exist at the time of writing and still does not exist twenty centuries later. All the same, Paul could see it with the eyes of faith and believed that it would come. He could picture it, even as I can occasionally picture my perfect garden.

Pause for Prayer

Take a walk just now around the garden of your life. Which are the neglected patches? Where are the places where the weeds seem to be choking off all the colour and promise? Invite God to walk around it with you, even as he used to walk in that first garden of old.

Dear God, forgive the disrepair into which this garden has fallen. Help me to see today just one bit which could be better with your hand upon it. Show me, Lord, and let's get to work. Amen.

Tale 28

A Drum is Not for Banging

More than a year had gone by since I had planted so many new plants under Henry's careful eye. Almost all had survived, and many had gone through their deep winter sleep and come back again. There was still plenty of room, though, and there were still all sorts of areas in the garden's canvas unpainted. The scope for buying such paint, though, was limited. With the country in tight lockdown, getting hold of plants was not easy. I had tried some by mail order, and the results had been patchy at best.

With that kind of inventiveness which is often born of tight circumstances, my mind reached out for the possibility of a 'project'. Sitting in my garage was a big wooden cable reel which Henry had asked me to store for him. Thankfully for me, he was not going to need it back, and so an idea was born. Now, before I tell you about that idea, I also need to remind you that DIY terrifies me. The son of a man who built furniture and constructed a car port from scratch, I have always lacked both confidence and skill in that department. If I fix a shelf, it will either be wonky, or flat once it has fallen to the floor. If I hang a drop of wallpaper, it is almost certain not to run parallel to all the others in the room. Practical projects and I do not mix.

However, somehow in the garden I am freed from the ghost of those particular failures. If a project goes wrong (and they do) it is outside, so I don't have to 'live with it' in the same way as I would in the house. With this in mind, I set to with my remaining sandpaper to prep my cable-reel 'coffee table'. I sanded it all down, coated the base and drum with two layers of decking stain and then painted an undercoat on the top. The latter dried in no time and was soon painted a lovely powder blue. The finishing touch was to add a very cheap art deco copper dish, which I had bought in an emporium, to the hole in the centre. It now sits at the bottom of the garden – a coffee table for me and an elegant bath for the birds!

Sometimes you have to see how a thing could be, before you can find it in yourself to start transforming it. I am convinced that God sees me that way. Hopefully, he sees more coffee table than empty cable drum when he looks in this direction.

Bible Reflection on Matthew 16:17–19

Peter the disciple was what you might have called 'a character'. He was all enthusiasm one minute and gloom the next. A few minutes after the words below, he would let Jesus down all over again and find himself rebuked as a result. All the same, Jesus could clearly see something very special in him:

> Jesus replied, 'Blessed are you, Simon son of Jonah, for this was not revealed to you by flesh and blood, but by my Father in heaven. And I tell you that you are Peter, and on this rock I will build my church, and the gates of Hades will not overcome it. I will give you the keys of the kingdom of heaven; whatever you bind on earth will be bound in heaven, and whatever you loose on earth will be loosed in heaven.'

Jesus was looking at Peter a bit like I looked at my cable drum – seeing the future glory rather than the current faults. I hope he does it with me too.

Pause for Prayer

Today would be a great day to thank God that he sees something positive in you. You don't need to know what it is – just to know that it is there. One day, perhaps, you will see it too, but for now it is his sight which matters.

> Dear God, will you help me to believe today that you can see some potential in me? I don't need to know what it is, but I do need to know that you see it. Thank you, my generous Father God. Amen.

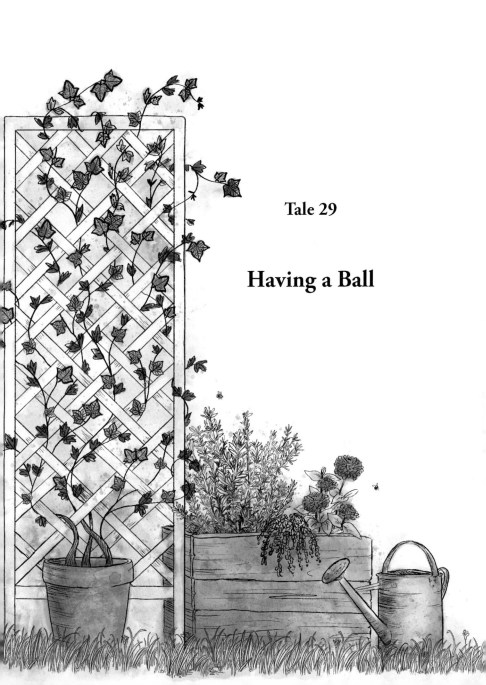

Tale 29

Having a Ball

I suppose at some point it was inevitable that two of my hobbies should converge. The love of photography was something that I inherited from my father. At the age of 8, I had my first ever 'proper' camera. It was a Russian-made twin lens reflex and took rolls of 120mm film, usually with twelve frames. Over the years, I learned all about exposure and aperture, learning to master depth of field and composition along the way. I even learned to mount the loft ladder, buckets in hand, to work in the darkroom we had there and produce prints and enlargements. That cumbersome 120mm camera gave way to a 35mm, and many years down the road that gave way to a digital SLR.

When 'project garden' came along, it was lovely to combine the two hobbies. My camera is never far away, whether that is to capture an autumn squirrel drinking from the birdbath, a dusting of frost round the wine-coloured leaves of the heucheras or the evening sunlight falling just so on the tall stems of the ornamental grasses. It has provided a good way to share the progress of 'project garden' with a wider audience too – especially with 'before' and 'after' pictures. One or two of my up-cycled projects have set creative hares off running in other minds and other gardens, I think.

Part way through my second year in the garden, I brought a new device to use with the camera. It is a clear glass sphere, 12 centimetres in diameter and known as a lens ball. Owing to the high quality of the glass, the lens ball will produce a beautiful, inverted representation of its surroundings, apparently sitting within the ball itself, as if inside a snow globe. Of course, it was not long before I started trying it in the garden. It was fun to try with big flowers bending across the inside of the globe. However, when I placed it in such a way that it captured almost a 360-degree view of the garden, including grass, flowers, trees and sky, it was something of a revelation to me. There, inside that perfect little globe, was everything I had been working on. It was all brought together as if in one little world. It made me feel inspired, awed and a little proprietorial, all at once.

Of course, very little of it was down to me. The blue arc of the sky had been put there by God, not me. The spectacular apple tree had been planted years and years before I ever came on the scene. The way the grasses grow, with their fronds shimmering on a summer's breeze, is all in the design, not the planting. All the same, it made me think about how God looks down at his little world.

Bible Reflection on Psalm 8

David was a king; within his own kingdom he had absolute authority to rule as he saw fit. Servants and slaves, soldiers and generals, were all at his beck and call. However, one of the lessons which the different chapters of his life had taught him was that God ultimately held everything in his hands:

> LORD, our Lord, how majestic is your name in all the earth! You have set your glory in the heavens. Through the praise of children and infants you have established a stronghold against your enemies, to silence the foe and the avenger. When I consider your heavens, the work of your fingers, the moon and the stars, which you have set in place, what is mankind that you are mindful of them, human beings that you care for them? You have made them a little lower than the angels and crowned them with glory and honour. You made them rulers over the works of your hands; you put everything under their feet: all flocks and herds, and the animals of the wild, the birds in the sky, and the fish in the sea, all that swim the paths of the seas. LORD, our Lord, how majestic is your name in all the earth!

The simplest and most profound lesson which 'project garden' has taught me has been to recognise the hand of God at work in creation.

Pause for Prayer

If you have access to one, then pick something from the garden before you pray today. It could be anything from a discarded leaf to a carefully selected rose. If you can't do that, then pick a tree, a plant, or patch of sky that you can see from the window. Let that thing be your inspiration to pray today.

> Dear God, I thank you for all the things you have made – the intricate and the simple, the enormous and the microscopic. Today, I thank you for this one thing which I have chosen. Help me to see your hand in it, I pray. Amen.

Tale 30

The Ill-prepared Pond

Months had gone by since my decking was finished, and I still had plenty of the thick damp-proof liner left over that I had bought for making 'hammocks' in my planters. All through the late autumn, cold winter and early spring it had sat in the shed. As you know, I had been well-schooled by my father in the philosophy of 'it might come in handy', so it had stayed there, folded and ready for action.

Now the summer was coming, and I sat down on a Saturday morning looking at a shady nook on the left-hand side of the garden. To one side rose a gorgeous buddleia tree – all gnarled boughs and beautiful purple flowers – and to the other, an apple tree and, behind that, the fence. This would never be a great patch for planting, as the shade was deep and the other plants hungrily sapped most of the moisture from the soil. There was another possibility, though – and that was a pond. I thumbed through my gardening books and flicked through some trusted websites on what to do, as I drank my coffee. My mind was made up – a pond it would be!

Coffee finished, I assembled my tools. Out of the shed came my trusty mattock, my shovel and my folded damp-proof liner. All morning I worked, filling one and two, then three and four wheelbarrows with soil, which I distributed elsewhere round the garden. The pond had an uneven shape, which I wanted, a gentle slope at one end and went down to about two-thirds of a metre deep in the centre. Before pausing for lunch, I lined the bottom with some old blankets, as instructed, and nodded approvingly at a good morning's work.

After lunch, I spread out the damp-proof liner, ready to snuggle it down into the pond. How my heart sank when I saw that it had not been alone all winter in the shed! Clearly the mice had been at it, and in places it looked more like a paper doily than a waterproof liner. Undeterred, I cut off the worst-affected bits and doubled up the rest in the hope that it would do. I began to run the water in gently from the hose – and the water rose, but only so far. After forty-five minutes, it was obvious that it simply would not do. I pulled off all the rocks which were pinning the liner down, pulled it out, and watched the water drain away into the soil. It was not the end of the project. I ordered some butyl liner which came the next week – and went through the whole lining and filling process all over again. The pond is now a treasured and tranquil place, sometimes full of soulful shadow and sometimes catching the light in dancing ripples. Only this week it has welcomed its first guest – a frog. All the same, every time I look at it, I remember my folly and a half-remembered phrase from my Cub Scout days about 'being prepared'.

Enthusiasm can be such a good thing, especially when we want to put it to good use for God and his kingdom. So often, though, I have tripped over my enthusiasm through a failure to plan – a bit like trying to run in giant clown shoes. Hopefully, I shall learn – but it might take a little while.

Bible Reflection on Luke 14:28–33

Jesus' parables seem to cover all manner of things – from domestic stories to matters of state. This particular saying could almost have been written for me and my pond:

> Suppose one of you wants to build a tower. Won't you first sit down and estimate the cost to see if you have enough money to complete it? For if you lay the foundation and are not able to finish it, everyone who sees it will ridicule you, saying, 'This person began to build and wasn't able to finish.' Or suppose a king is about to go to war against another king. Won't he first sit down and consider whether he is able with ten thousand men to oppose the one coming against him with twenty thousand? If he is not able, he will send a delegation while the other is still a long way off and will ask for terms of peace. In the same way, those of you who do not give up everything you have cannot be my disciples.

Of course, the real point here is about something far more profound than ponds, towers or wars. Those of us who intend to follow Jesus must be prepared to do so – when things succeed and when they fail.

Pause for Prayer

Why not reflect today in God's presence on something which did not go to plan? It might have been a perfectly good idea, but somehow it never came off. To acknowledge that, and to let go of the pain associated with it, can be such a good thing.

> Dear God, here are my failed plans, spread out before you like a child's story, all covered in crossings-out. Help me to remember today that you understand both intent and execution, or the lack of it. I leave them both with you. Amen.

Tale 31

Broken but Beautiful

What a strange turn of events this was proving to be! As a man who had scarcely darkened the doors of a nursery and rarely entered a DIY shop, these days I was doing both. As the garden project advanced, I seemed to be constantly in and out of my local garden and DIY shop. To start with, I would load up the car with sacks and sacks of bark chippings. Each one would scarcely seem to cover any of my newly cleared ground, and so I would go back for more. Then there was that strip of gravel in front of the old, neglected pergola, and I bought white gypsum to liven it up. Of course, I bought only half of what I needed and had to go back. I bought tools too. I bought the tools that any gardener would need. Unfortunately, they were not all tools which this gardener needed as it turned out.

Then, disaster struck. With very little warning, the shop announced that it was closing down. I bought all sorts there – from parasols to wire netting and trellises. On the last day of trading, I spotted a rattan chair in a heap of neglected goods. It was fraying a little round the edges but still appeared serviceable. I asked the cashier how much it was, and he wearily shrugged his shoulders and suggested a fiver. I was happy to comply. As it turned out, it was not the bargain it seemed. To have one odd chair with my others looked, not surprisingly, odd. Furthermore, the rattan that was unravelling from the arms was in a continuous thread with the seat. It would be only a matter of time before the whole thing would be dangerous to sit upon. I added it to a pile of oddities in my garage and considered it a fiver ill spent.

The following summer, I was looking for a new project, and the chair caught my eye. I had a little more gardening experience by now.

Furthermore, the garden was teaching me to banish some of my DIY demons. The son of a brilliant carpenter, I had inherited none of my father's skill – you are familiar now with my fear of any DIY project. Somehow, though, it didn't seem to matter so much in the garden. After all, if it went wrong here, who was going to see it, apart from the dog and me? In that spirit, I decided to tackle the chair. I removed the seat completely, resulting in a pile of discarded staples and rattan on the floor. Next, I created a planting pocket where the seat had once been. I perforated that shallow pocket with little holes and then painted the remaining back of the chair a powder blue and left it to dry in the hot sunshine. Later, a trip to the garden centre brought me home with a tray of alpines and some horticultural grit. By the time the sun set on that day, my chair had become a miniature garden, with pink and green houseleeks set among a miniature rocky landscape. Some of them were *Sempervivum arachnoideum*, or 'cobweb' houseleeks, and simply added to the intrigue of this quirky little garden.

For me, one of the most precious aspects of the Christian faith is the persistence of God. Long after I would have given up, God is still finding ways to bless, to heal and to offer redemption. He loves to give a second chance, a bit like I did with my throwaway chair.

Bible Reflection on Hosea 11:7–9

There are some moments in the Bible where the real compassion of God shows through, like a rocky outcrop poking out through grass. This one, in the book of Hosea, is one of them. You can almost feel the raw emotion:

> My people are determined to turn from me. Even though they call me God Most High, I will by no means exalt them. How can I give you up, Ephraim? How can I hand you over, Israel? How can I treat you like Admah? How can I make you like Zeboyim? My heart is changed within me; all my compassion is aroused. I will not carry out my fierce anger, nor will I devastate Ephraim again.

God does not give up, which is just as well.

 **Pause for Prayer**

Do you ever look in the mirror and think, 'If I were God, I wouldn't bother'? Or maybe that is only me! Every once in a while, it is worth stopping and dwelling on this one amazing fact – that God does not give up on any of us.

> Dear God, I thank you today that you look at me and see what could be, rather than what is. Thank you that you see the flourishing garden instead of the broken chair. Today, I ask that you might help me to see that too. Amen.

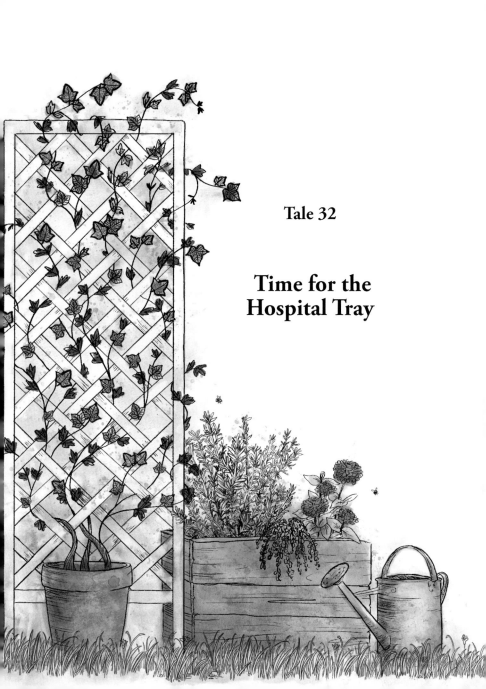

Tale 32

Time for the
Hospital Tray

By this stage, I was into my second summer of gardening and loving every minute of it. I loved it when things went well, of course. To see a plant which I had planted in its infancy come back for a second summer and bloom again was a tremendous encouragement. With seedlings, that feeling was multiplied several-fold. I could not quite believe that some tiny dots which I had shaken into my hand and pushed into warm earth had rewarded my labours by pushing up to greet God's warm sun. When their leaves unfurled and their colourful flowers came, it took my breath away.

Strangely enough, I was quite enjoying it when things did not work too. Early on, I learned that watering my spectacular 'Golden Dream' berberis when the sun was shining was a silly thing to do. Each droplet of water settled on those gorgeous golden leaves and acted like a tiny lens. The sun, focused through the lens, was burning the leaves and killing the plant. I soon changed the way I watered it. I learned that plants could be moved too. If I had put them too close together or in a spot which was too shady, it *was* possible to move them as long as it was done gently. If ever it did not work, a lesson had been learned and I would plant a new one somewhere else another time.

With the summer of my second year came a new project. Inspired by other creative ideas I had seen, I decided to convert an old forklift pallet into a planter. It didn't take long to find one for free, so I brought it home and began the conversion. Two of the slats were removed and fixed behind to create shelves. The whole thing was then painted my beloved powder blue, and I ended up with a rough and ready planter with three shelves. Into it went purple sweet williams, begonias and geraniums. The effect of the red flowers, especially, against the rough blue wood was very pleasing – and caused many passers-by to stop and look at it in my front garden. All was not well, though. It was hard for water to penetrate through from the top shelf to the ones below, and my flowers began to look very sorry for themselves.

At this point, I remembered those long-forgotten trips to the nursery mentioned in 'Hidden Threads' and bought myself what would come to be known as the 'hospital tray'. It was just a simple, shallow black plastic tray about 70 × 30 centimetres, but it would prove to be a lifeline for my flowers. Every once in a while, I would remove three or four plants from the pallet and stand them in the tray full of water overnight. In this way, they could get the 'good long drink' of which my parents used to speak. Water falling from a watering can or hose, or even from the sky, could bounce off the hard earth of those little pots. Soaking it up through their roots at their own pace was a different matter entirely and would often haul my plants back from the brink.

As a pastor, I have always believed that exposure to the Bible is as vital to any life as water is to a plant. However, simply 'firing' it at people can be as harmful as squirting a hose at my tired little plants. People need time to absorb the depth and richness of God's Word at their own pace if they are to flourish.

Bible Reflection on 2 Peter 1:3,4

Peter was a disciple who blew hot and cold – a bit like my flowers, sometimes flourishing and sometimes wilting. He was quite capable of lurching from great wisdom and insight one minute to downright folly the next. However, by the time he wrote his letters, he was looking back on many years of serving Jesus and had learned many lessons. Read these words, as he writes to fellow Christians in his second letter:

> His divine power has given us everything we need for a godly life through our knowledge of him who called us by his own glory and goodness. Through these he has given us his very great and precious promises . . .

We have all we need in his Word. The sum total of all his promises is enough to sustain life and faith for as long as it is needed. Whenever we are weary, we need to make our way to the 'hospital tray' and soak them up all over again.

Pause for Prayer

Do you feel dry and thirsty? Do you look at other Christians and feel that their faith is in full flower whilst your leaves are curling with thirst? It happens to all of us at some stage, and there is no shame in it. When we see it, though, we need to take some time in the 'hospital tray' to soak up all God's goodness from his promises.

Dear God, I feel so dry and weary today. I know there are things I ought to tackle and lessons I ought to learn. For today, though, could I just soak my roots in all that goodness of your promises of old? Tomorrow, I'll do some growing – but today I need to rest. Amen.

Tale 33

The Huffy Hellebore

Despite what I said in the previous chapter about moving plants, it does not always work out for the best. When I first started on the garden, I was keen to find out about plants which would thrive in shade. I am fortunate enough to have established trees to the right and left of my garden. They provide dappled shade across the centre of the garden, and the sound of their leaves rustling in a summer breeze is one which I savour. However, they do create problems. Their roots crop up in all sorts of places where you would least expect them when digging holes to plant something new. They suck up much of the moisture from the soil, and they create deep shade immediately beneath their branches.

Many of those plants which thrive in shade, I discovered, are ones with pale blooms. This trait enables them to attract insects even in a shady setting, as the pale petals stand out. A classic example of this is the hellebore, often found with petals of white or the palest green. I hoovered up this information and planted three of them in my first summer, knowing that I would not really see their value until early spring the following year. All through the autumn, they hunkered down and did nothing, often disappearing beneath the carpet of leaves. In winter, the tree leaves had gone, and the leaves of the hellebores often bore a dusting of frost and were occasionally bowed under snow. Sure enough, though, when spring came, they began to flower. Their lovely blooms seemed like an act of defiance against all the dullness of hefty autumn days and all the harshness of winter.

When the second summer came, though, it was time to move one of them. When the pond was being made, I needed to relocate one of my faithful hellebores. I lifted it carefully, making sure to retain a good clump of soil around the root-ball. Its new home was in a patch of garden where the soil had been improved and the shade was a little lighter. It seemed to me that there was nothing not to love about it. The hellebore, though, seemed not to agree. It is still alive, but it droops as if in a state of permanent dejection. It was only later that an older and wiser gardener told me that they are a plant which 'does not like' to be moved. If only I had known!

My years of pastoral ministry have taught me again and again that people do not always liked to be moved either. Of course, they *can* be, just like the hellebore *could* be – but they may not thrive. Changes in the church environment – whether of layout or music, or even who sits where, can evoke a similar reaction to the one displayed by my hellebore.

There are times when we need to be moved, but we do not always enjoy it.

Bible Reflection on Psalm 137:1–6

Being uprooted is never easy, as my hellebore would tell you if it could speak. In Psalm 137, the writer recalls a testing moment in his people's history. Long before we had heard the phrase 'ethnic cleansing', the ancient Babylonians were employing it. They uprooted the Jewish people en masse and deposited them in refugee camps along the River Tigris. Here the psalmist recalls how it felt but also insists on the instincts of faith:

> By the rivers of Babylon we sat and wept when we remembered Zion. There on the poplars we hung our harps, for there our captors asked us for songs, our tormentors demanded songs of joy; they said, 'Sing us one of the songs of Zion!' How can we sing the songs of the LORD while in a foreign land? If I forget you, Jerusalem, may my right hand forget its skill. May my tongue cling to the roof of my mouth if I do not remember you, if I do not consider Jerusalem my highest joy.

In essence, the psalmist is saying that it was fine to pine for the things and places they had left behind – but that their pining should not silence the voice of faith. It is still so.

Pause for Prayer

Is there a person or a place which you are missing terribly? Do you feel a twinge of pain which is almost physical whenever you think of them? God, who created you, is not in the least bit surprised by such a response. What matters is not whether we feel these things or not – but what we do with the feelings.

Dear God, you know how my heart fills with pain whenever I think of this. You know how it brings the darkest cloud across the horizon, and I feel that I cannot see the sun. Today, I ask only that you stay close by my side until the cloud has passed. Amen.

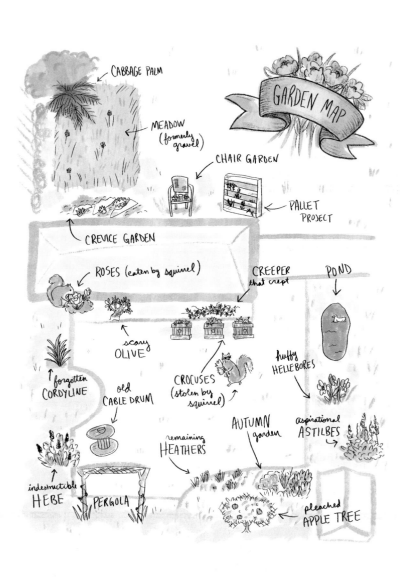

CABBAGE PALM

MEADOW
(formerly gravel)

GARDEN MAP

CHAIR GARDEN

PALLET PROJECT

CREVICE GARDEN

ROSES (eaten by squirrel)

CREEPER that crept

POND

scary OLIVE

CROCUSES (stolen by squirrel)

huffy HELLEBORES

↑ forgotten CORDYLINE

old CABLE DRUM

remaining HEATHERS

AUTUMN garden

aspirational ASTILBES

indestructible HEBE

PERGOLA

pleached APPLE TREE

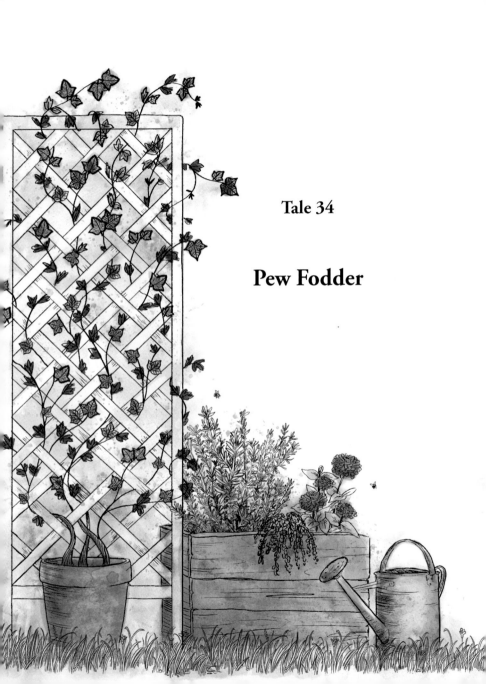

Tale 34

Pew Fodder

Some time, long before I came to this house, a pew came to stay. The church was swapping pews for chairs, and one or two of them found new homes. I know that because I have seen them. One of them, a rather dainty little half-pew, sits in the porchway of an elegant bungalow just up the road. It has been treated and varnished and polished and looks as good as new. Mine could not be described as dainty. Never designed to be outside, of course, the years and the weather have taken their toll. Half of the footrail is missing, and the other half is attached at one end only, leaving it drooping to the ground, as if feeling for support. Years of damp have found their way inside the woodwork, and the whole thing is now bent at what would be a very precarious angle if anyone should attempt to sit upon it. It is unlikely that they will, though. The seat now curves downwards and would probably snap off if any vigorous sitting were to happen.

That said, I love this old pew. It is a reminder that this is not just any house but a manse. It is a house bought by the generosity of people of faith to provide a roof over the head of their pastor. Unable to restore the pew properly, I decided to sand and paint it. When I did so, the white of the primer I had used showed through the powder blue of the top coat. It gave it a look somewhere between 'shabby chic' and 'weather-beaten beach hut' and simply added to its charm. Was there more that I could do with it, though? That is where the idea of the hymnbook shelf was born.

Using my newly emerging DIY skills, I divided the shelf into two sections, using thick batons at each end. I then fixed damp-proof liner into place to create two planting pockets, perforated them with holes for drainage and hoped for the best. Into my little pockets went some rich compost, a mix of 'bee-friendly' flowers and a lot of optimism. When summer came, so did the seedlings, and my pew took on an air of almost seaside gaiety. The seeds were probably not the best, as they grew tall, and the small amount of soil in the pocket was not enough to really sustain them. All the same, they shot up and danced in the summer breezes in all their pinks, purples, yellows and oranges. Looking at them, I reflected how once upon a time, a hymnbook might have lain on that shelf, open at the page for 'All Things Bright and Beautiful'. Now it was those very things which occupied the space.

God has a habit of taking those things which are past their best, or overlooked, and turning them into something better. There is a dark and desolate place in the story of Joshua where a terrible thing happens, and it gets named 'Achor' or 'desolation' (Josh. 7:24). Years later, it gets renamed by the prophet Hosea as 'a door of hope' (Hos. 2:15). What a transformation!

I think Joshua would have liked my pew.

Bible Reflection on Luke 15:17–24

The story of the 'prodigal son' is probably one of the best-known Bible stories in the world. In it, a headstrong young man leaves his father's house with a pocket full of money and little common sense. He spends his money foolishly, falls on hard times and becomes a shadow of his former self. The moment when he comes home and embraces his waiting father is one to savour:

> When he came to his senses, he said, 'How many of my father's hired servants have food to spare, and here I am starving to death! I will set out and go back to my father and say to him: Father, I have sinned against heaven and against you. I am no longer worthy to be called your son; make me like one of your hired servants.' So he got up and went to his father. But while he was still a long way off, his father saw him and was filled with compassion for him; he ran to his son, threw his arms round him and kissed him. "The son said to him, 'Father, I have sinned against heaven and against you. I am no longer worthy to be called your son.' But the father said to his servants, 'Quick! Bring the best robe and put it on him. Put a ring on his finger and sandals on his feet. Bring the fattened calf and kill it. Let's have a feast and celebrate. For this son of mine was dead and is alive again; he was lost and is found.' So they began to celebrate.

I'm not sure that my pew is exactly 'prodigal', but I do love that fact that it has had a second chance. God has given many of those to me, thank goodness.

Pause for Prayer

Is there a person on whom you have felt tempted to give up? You don't want to, of course, it's just that you can't seem to get through. Or maybe there has been some good thing you have been prompted time and time again to do – but you just haven't done it yet. Remember my old broken pew, and ask God to help you do something positive today.

Dear God, today I ask that you might give me the strength I need to do this good thing. Give me the eyes of faith to see what could be, rather than what is, I pray. Amen.

Tale 35

The Orphan Tree

Given how little experience I have as a gardener, I really shouldn't do it. The thing is, I just can't help myself. Whenever I am in a garden centre, I am drawn to what I call the 'hospital shelf'. On it are the rejects, always reduced in price, which are imperfect in some way. Sometimes the pot is damaged, or a stem has been snapped off. Other times, it is a little more drastic than that. These plants are on their way to the compost bin if someone doesn't snap them up. Quite often, that someone is me. I take them home, water them, plant them, mulch them and hope for the best. Most times it works. I have a planter with a spreading carpet of ajuga which had all but shrivelled during the long months of lockdown in 2020. I have an amusingly named 'Torbay Dazzler' cordyline, which looked ready to give up for months, but now lights up a corner of my front garden. That said, I also had some tired begonias which were weary when I bought them and hopeless when I gave up on them.

All of my 'rescue' plants to date have been small and unassuming. However, when I saw a beautiful acer on the 'hospital shelf', my heart was drawn to it. Some of the branches had been snapped through careless handling or wind damage. There were only a few tiny leaves clinging to it here and there. Those leaves, though, were already showing the delicate edges and range of colours for which these Japanese maples are famous. The undamaged stems had a beautiful grey-green bark, and I felt there was still hope. To date, that hope is still alive. I brought it home, soaked it in water overnight and trimmed back the most damaged branches. I then planted it in a well-drained pot, fed it with some very diluted plant food and waited. The pot is placed in a spot which is sheltered from the wind but which gets a good few hours of sun each day. More importantly, though, it is near the back door. I cannot go into the garden without passing my little rescued tree, and that is the way I like it. Of course, my attention in itself can do nothing to make it thrive, but I choose to believe that it helps.

Actually, that is not quite true. I am sure my attention does nothing to help the plant – but it does a lot to help me. Gardening has affected the plot of land surrounding my house, of course. However, the impact on the person tending it has been greater still. I have always enjoyed God's creation and have been known to preach sermons on it, especially at harvest time. Now, though, it is personal. The 'big theology' of creation and redemption has been writ small in my little potted tree. An arc of theology, which stretches far too wide and high above my head for me to focus upon, comes into sharp relief within the confines of this little pot.

There is a point, I believe, in every Christian life, where the big story of God's intentions for humankind must be seen in this life or that. A bit like me and my little acer, it all becomes personal. The Bible abounds with God using terms like 'orphan' or 'lamb' or 'child' for those whom he protects. Maybe I am starting to understand that just a little more now.

Bible Reflection on Matthew 13:44-46

The idea of the kingdom of God had been around for a long time before Jesus walked the earth. Prophets of old had written about the 'Day of the Lord', when God's rule would stretch, unhindered, across the earth. Jesus announced the arrival of a 'kingdom of God', where a similar thing would happen. For now, that kingdom remained only subtly present and was there for the keen eyes of faith to spot.

> The kingdom of heaven is like treasure hidden in a field. When a man found it, he hid it again, and then in his joy went and sold all he had and bought that field. Again, the kingdom of heaven is like a merchant looking for fine pearls. When he found one of great value, he went away and sold everything he had and bought it.

If my little acer should survive, and if it should flourish, I know that I shall feel a thrill entirely disproportionate either to the plant itself or to the price I paid for it. I like to feel that on the day the kingdom comes, God will feel the same way about me.

Pause for Prayer

Take some time today to reflect on the miraculous way in which we sometimes stumble across faith. It can be like me unearthing that little tree from the hospital shelf – tipped over on its side and broken. Remember that God was looking for you for far longer than you were looking for him.

Dear God, I thank you that you found me. I thank you, too, that you could see past the outside to all that I could be. I know I am not there yet, and there are so many imperfections, but I thank you that this particular rescue project is under way. Maybe today I will grow a new leaf or two. Amen.

Tale 36

New Life for Old

It was the lockdown summer of 2020, and I had spent many happy hours in the back garden. To say that it was anywhere near finished would have been a lie. In fact, I doubt there is a gardener alive who would ever say that their garden is finished, since that is part of the joy of them. However, there was not much further I could go until plants started establishing themselves. This being so, I turned my attention to the front garden.

Of course, that front garden had already changed, with the addition of the meadow instead of the gravel. The trouble is, my view of it was obscured. With many hours now spent in my home office, I wanted to be able to look out on those waving fronds. There was a problem, though – an old forsythia bush. It was gangly and a terrible thief of my light! Although it regularly had sprays of bright yellow flowers, there was not much else to commend it. After taking a deep breath, I decided to get rid of it and replace it with something else. I started off with the secateurs, clipping away at the branches so that I could get at the main trunk. Even as those golden flowers fell to the ground, I wondered whether I was doing the right thing.

When I got down to trying to remove the roots, my doubts about the whole thing grew. I went through fork, spade, saw and mattock in the blazing sun of a June morning before finally wresting the last of the forsythia from its home. Now I was left with an ugly scar under my window. Had this all been a hot-headed mistake? Not pausing to reflect for too long, I started barrowing soil and gravel from the back garden. I started off with weed-proof membrane and then layered soil and gravel until I had built up a mound of the proportions I had imagined. It was to be a *crevice* garden, with rocks laid vertically like the strata on a mountainside.

A crevice garden is a good way to preserve moisture for alpine plants, as their roots can go deep. Another advantage of the crevice garden was that it would use materials I had lying around the garden already. I took great glee in breaking up old flagstones and concrete slabs, which I had found lying in the bottom of the garden, for this project. By dropping them to break them unevenly, I got a very pleasing effect overall.

After this, and a trip to the garden centre for horticultural grit, compost and dwarf alpines, I was ready to get started. I had a selection of sedums, houseleeks, rock poppies and the amusingly named shoehorn plant – with fleshy leaves in the shape of a shoehorn. Some thrived, others failed, and over time I opted for the more robust varieties rather than the spindly thrift and rock poppies. As I look out at it now, the plants are starting to clamber pleasingly over the broken flagstones, and there is a carpet of sedum tumbling down the side of this artificial little mountain slope. Maybe it was worth getting rid of that forsythia after all.

Relinquishing that which is good enough for that which could be even better is the constant tug-of-war at the heart of faith. Moses encountered it early on when people looked wistfully back over their shoulders at the land of Egypt (Exod. 14:11). They might have been slaves there, but at least they were fed. What had they done, leaving it all behind? Peter felt a little pang of it, when he realised that accepting Jesus' call to follow him would mean that he would have to be a witness to Jesus' dramatic downfall and execution (Matt. 16:22). Churches realise it when they abandon a building which is draughty and tired but tolerable, for one which could offer so much more. The period whilst they are homeless, or lodging temporarily in a school hall, can give plenty of scope for doubts to creep in.

Bible Reflection on Matthew 14:22–31

Peter the disciple, and later the apostle, is a glorious mixture of faith and doubt, courage and fear. One minute he can be striding forth like a lion-hearted leader, and the next, cowering from the consequences of his own folly. In this passage, he does something incredibly brave – walking on water – but all does not go to plan:

> Immediately Jesus made the disciples get into the boat and go on ahead of him to the other side, while he dismissed the crowd. After he had dismissed them, he went up on a mountainside by himself to pray. Later that night, he was there alone, and the boat was already a considerable distance from land, buffeted by the waves because the wind was against it. Shortly before dawn Jesus went out to them, walking on the lake. When the disciples saw him walking on the lake, they were terrified. 'It's a ghost,' they said, and cried out in fear. But Jesus immediately said to them: 'Take courage! It is I. Don't be afraid.' 'Lord, if it's you,' Peter replied, 'tell me to come to you on the water.' 'Come,' he said. Then Peter got down out of the boat, walked on the water and came towards Jesus. But when he saw the wind, he was afraid and, beginning to sink, cried out, 'Lord, save me!' Immediately Jesus reached out his hand and caught him. 'You of little faith,' he said, 'why did you doubt?

Did you see the moment when Peter had his wobble? In asking Jesus to command him out of the boat and across the water he was doing something which no human being had ever done before. Not only that, but it was something which none of his fellow disciples were prepared to do. He was starting so well. Then the doubts kicked in, the fear began to rise and the inevitable happened. Thank goodness for the outstretched hand of Jesus to help him.

Pause for Prayer

Have you bitten off more than you can chew? Have you embarked on a project or a scheme driven by faith, but now you are wondering whether it was right in the first place? Are you looking down at the severed flowers of that forsythia, wondering whether it might not have been better to leave well alone? Talk to God about it, right now. Hand over that tangled ball of faith and doubt which we all know so well, and let him unravel it.

> Dear God, you know I had all the right reasons for starting on this, but now I can't see the end. I feel stuck – as if I can't go back but don't want to go on. Give me the gifts of both clarity and strength today, I pray. Amen.

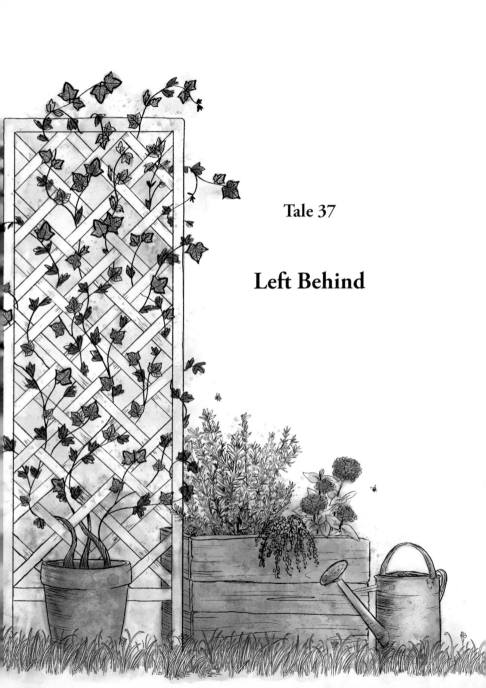

Tale 37

Left Behind

My feeling about leaves in the garden changes with the seasons. In the spring they lift my spirits. The appearance of them on the apple tree and the buddleia signal the start of something wonderful. The earth is warming up, the bulbs are unfurling and soon it will be safe to plant all sorts of seeds with their promise of new life. In summer, they provide a canopy above my head. One of my favourite sounds in the garden is to hear the leaves rustle in a summer's breeze. There is something innately soothing about it, I find. In early autumn, the leaves really start to come into their own – starting with the Virginia creeper and working round to the bigger trees; a symphony of yellows, golds, scarlet and even crimson as the colours begin to change. Mind you, it also signals a lot of work, as the battle to keep the leaves swept up and away from smothering the smaller plants begins. By winter, that job is almost done. The only foliage left is on the evergreens. My smoke bush, or *Cotinus coggyria*, keeps its leaves – but they are a coppery colour and stand out alone. In due course, the whole cycle will begin again.

Sometimes, though, there is one which breaks the cycle. On this occasion I found the remains of an autumn leaf on a dry, hot summer's day. One of the legacies that my paternal grandmother bequeathed to me was a fascination with tiny things in nature – and this particular leaf was one of them. By the time I picked it up on that blistering summer day, the parts of its surface which remained were rough and papery. What was left behind, though, was a leaf skeleton of exquisite complexity and beauty. Even with a garden full of summer colour all around, I took this leaf away to a spot where I could photograph it against a plain white background. I tried it this way and that, noting how the shadows changed with the angle. For those few moments I was pleased to ignore all the flowers and all the landscaping which I had invested in the garden. I was happy to leave it all on one side that I might marvel at this tiny miracle in which I had played no part at all.

When you are new to gardening, like me, you tend to consume a lot of gardening books. Many of them talk about the importance of planning. They say that you should have an overall idea of how your garden will look and a picture of how it will change with the seasons. Many extol the value of bulk planting, so that you can create drifts of colour and shape to please the eye. I agree with all of that, but if I ever lose the ability to stop and gaze at some tiny part of all that natural wonder, then I've a feeling I will have missed the point.

As a preacher, and a teacher of other preachers, I often emphasise the need to see the big picture. A saying of Jesus or one of his stories, for instance, should not be understood simply in the context of the page on which it sits. It is woven into a much bigger tapestry of God's purposes, stretching all the way back to the first moment of creation and all the way forward to the New Jerusalem. Context is everything. Or is it? Sometimes, like with a little discarded leaf skeleton, we need to stop, turn over a small gem of God's wisdom in our hearts and savour it for its own sake.

Bible Reflection on Psalm 139:7–18

We can see the biblical character of David as many things. He is shepherd boy and king. He is soldier and musician. He is poet and giant-killer. He is wise teacher and foolish sinner. All these things are true. Psalm 139, though, gives us the greatest clue as to how he sees himself:

> Where can I go from your Spirit? Where can I flee from your presence? If I go up to the heavens, you are there; if I make my bed in the depths, you are there. If I rise on the wings of the dawn, if I settle on the far side of the sea, even there your hand will guide me, your right hand will hold me fast. If I say, 'Surely the darkness will hide me and the light become night around me,' even the darkness will not be dark to you; the night will shine like the day, for darkness is as light to you. For you created my inmost being; you knit me together in my mother's womb. I praise you because I am fearfully and wonderfully made; your works are wonderful, I know that full well. My frame was not hidden from you when I was made in the secret place, when I was woven together in the depths of the earth. Your eyes saw my unformed body; all the days ordained for me were written in your book before one of them came to be. How precious to me are your thoughts, God! How vast is the sum of them! Were I to count them, they would outnumber the grains of sand – when I awake, I am still with you.

In these moments he is neither king nor champion nor giant-killer. In these moments, he is human – the crown of God's creation.

Pause for Prayer

Some days you have so many things going round in your head that it is hard to stop and look at any single one of them. They might all be good things – it is just that there are so many. Choose just one now – like me picking out my leaf skeleton from the thousands of leaves in the garden. Choose it, hold it and tell God all about it.

Well, Lord, here it is. Here's the one thing which I have picked out from all the many buzzing round in my head today. Help me to see it for what it is worth and to be grateful, I pray. Amen.

Tale 38

Outdoors Indoors

I have always resisted the idea of having plants in the house – and with good reason. I am blessed with an inherent capacity to kill them through neglect. When Fiona and I first married, we moved into our little terraced house two doors down from the church. Lots of people came to greet the new assistant pastor and his wife, and many brought gifts. As it turns out, three of them brought a yellow chrysanthemum. We nodded and smiled and thanked them for their gift, all the while wondering how we would keep this latest addition alive. In the end, we had to resort to subterfuge. Whichever was the healthiest-looking at the time when the relevant donor returned would be brought into the front room. This way, it could be noticed (even if not admired) and honour was maintained. Of course, the scheme was flawed – and in the end, time and neglect caught up with all three plants. The yellow chrysanthemums were no more.

My current house remained entirely houseplant-free until the late summer of 2020. By then, I had invested time, care and energy in pots and pots of geraniums which had adorned my blue pallet and run along the wall beside it. I was expecting to consign them to the compost heap, as I had done at the close of the previous year. However, another gardener told me that there was no need to do so. 'Bring them inside for the winter,' she said. 'They'll be fine.' I was very sceptical about the whole idea until she also mentioned that, once indoors, they could be pretty much neglected, with just an occasional watering. That sounded manageable, even for me. I started to look around for a plant stand or something similar on which I could place them in my dining room, next to a big window.

All this coincided with the arrival of a new desk. Home-working was now set to continue for many months, and so I needed to improve my work environment. The old desk on which I had been working hitherto had been a throwaway from a neighbour. It was bashed, battered and too low down. With the new one in place, I took the old one outside to dismantle it, ready for disposal. That was when I had the idea to make a stand for the geraniums. Using my hesitant skills but spurred on by the thought that few people would see my handiwork, I made two plinths, stacked on top of each other, on which the plants could be stored. The metalwork didn't go to waste either, but that is a story for another chapter.

The plinths came in, the plants went on and a strange thing began to happen. I had chosen these plants. I had watered and dead-headed them all through the summer. They stood now on a wooden plinth that I had made for them. In no time at all, I started to really care about them. Never mind the regime of near neglect that I had been expecting. I took off the dead leaves regularly, I watered them whenever needed and I kept turning them so that they grew evenly. My old yellow chrysanthemums would have been astonished!

When we join a church, either as pastor or member, we don't get to choose all the people who are in it. Many of them were there long before us, and we simply have to accept it. The Bible tells us that they are like 'brothers and sisters' (Rom. 8:29) to us, but they may not truly feel that way. However, over time a curious thing begins to happen. Oddly, it is a process which is accelerated by adversity. As we weather the storms together, we begin to find that we start to see each other differently. This man starts to feel like a brother and that woman starts to feel like a sister. We are drawn into a family whose roots run deeper than biology. Despite ourselves, we end up caring very deeply.

Bible Reflection on Romans 16:3–16

As a pastor, I often wish I had an outstanding memory for names and faces. Sadly, it is not so. One of the advantages of doing church by video call, when it came to that, was that each person had their name displayed beneath their face. If only they had it all the time. As Paul travelled round the ancient world planting churches, his list of names to remember must have grown longer and longer. Most of us skip over lists of names in the Bible, but I urge you not to do so with this one. As you read it, note how Paul addresses each person differently and finds something to value in each one:

> Greet Priscilla and Aquila, my fellow workers in Christ Jesus. They risked their lives for me. Not only I but all the churches of the Gentiles are grateful to them. Greet also the church that meets at their house. Greet my dear friend Epenetus, who was the first convert to Christ in the province of Asia. Greet Mary, who worked very hard for you. Greet Andronicus and Junia, my fellow Jews who have been in prison with me. They are outstanding among the apostles, and they were in Christ before I was. Greet Ampliatus, my dear friend in the Lord. Greet Urbanus, our fellow worker in Christ, and my dear friend Stachys. Greet Apelles, whose fidelity to Christ has stood the test. Greet those who belong to the household of Aristobulus. Greet Herodion, my fellow Jew. Greet those in the household of Narcissus who are in the Lord. Greet Tryphena and Tryphosa, those women who work hard in the Lord. Greet my

dear friend Persis, another woman who has worked very hard in the Lord. Greet Rufus, chosen in the Lord, and his mother, who has been a mother to me, too. Greet Asyncritus, Phlegon, Hermes, Patrobas, Hermas and the other brothers and sisters with them. Greet Philologus, Julia, Nereus and his sister, and Olympas and all the Lord's people who are with them. Greet one another with a holy kiss.

This is a man who cherishes the people whom God has given to him.

Pause for Prayer

Try to picture some of the people who have had an influence on your Christian life. As they come to mind, some will have names attached and others not. Don't worry about that just now. Simply allow them to walk into your imagination and stay there for a minute or two.

Dear God, I thank you for these people. I thank you for their gifts and their faith. If there are some whom I have not truly valued, then I ask you to pick out just one now, that I might pray for them. Amen.

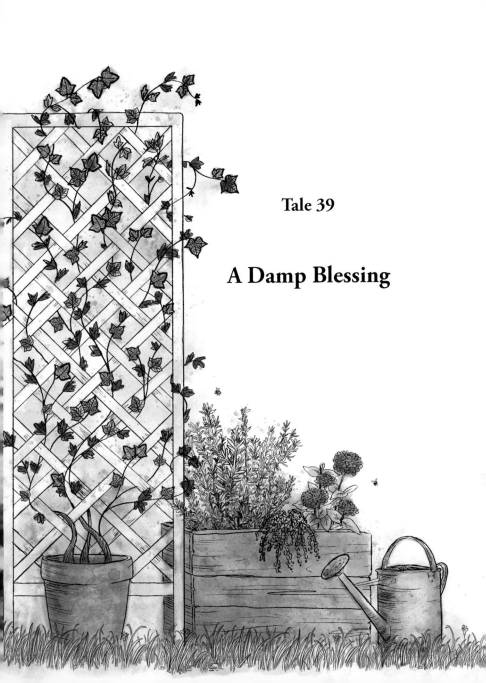

Tale 39

A Damp Blessing

I had been looking forward to it all year, and then I missed it. I had watched, with a growing sense of anticipation as summer's fingers stretched out long into September, as if clinging on to a ledge and unwilling to let go. There was no doubt about it, though; autumn was coming. Already, there had been a morning or two with a cold nip in the air and tufts of mist rolling across the fields. Then, just as the conductor tapped his baton on the rostrum ready for it all to begin – I had to leave. An emergency meant that I was needed on the other side of the world, so I jumped on a plane.

When I came back ten days later, autumn had taken up residence. Leaves were turning on the trees, summer blooms were curling up and fluttering away from the plants and it had rained and rained and rained. Dusty earth had turned a deep, chestnut brown, and the last of the apples were clinging to the very top of the tree. Something else had happened in my absence, though. It was an unexpected and wonderful transformation. Around the garden, and especially in the areas of greatest shade and damp, something new had appeared. There were hundreds and hundreds of toadstools. Some were off-white, others a deep burnt sienna in colour. Some had a tinge of yellow to the edge of their caps, and others looked like tiny parasols. I had never seen anything like it before and kept going back to the garden again and again with my camera. It felt like autumn had laid on a party for the absent guest.

One of the things that gardening has taught me is an appreciation of the bounty of God's creation. It is more than that, though. I had done nothing of any kind to bring about this latest wave of beauty in the garden. I had not planted, tended, weeded or watered to make it happen. These hundreds of tiny, perfect fungi had appeared entirely of their own accord, and all I needed to do was enjoy them. They were a multi-stemmed, soft-capped, spore-driven picture of grace, and I loved it.

Not only this, but their rich, earthy colours meant that I did not spot them all at once. Every time I visited a new corner of the garden to see what had grown up or died back in my absence and bent down to see what was going on, I got a surprise. It seemed that they were there in every corner – tall, short, dark, light and everything in between. Like the blessings of God, they were both surprising and multifaceted.

Bible Reflection on 1 Peter 4:10

I like Peter. I love his enthusiasm, and I love his uncanny ability to put his foot in his mouth. As a person who occasionally speaks up first and realises the consequences second, I can identify with this. All the same, Jesus thought Peter was the right kind of person on which to build a church for sinners. Maybe his combination of faith and folly was thought to be the perfect one? Years after Christ had originally chosen him, when he was already an established figure in the early church, Peter wrote to others to urge them to get fully involved in the kingdom. In 1 Peter 4:10, he urges them to serve as:

> . . . faithful stewards of God's grace *in its various forms*. (emphasis mine)

The words emphasised above are just one word in the original Greek text, which could be translated as 'multi-coloured'. I love that description of God's 'rainbow grace'. Like my fungi cropping up in all different corners in all shapes and sizes – so we find the grace of God, even in the darker corners.

Pause for Prayer

As you look out on your life right now, do you see darker corners where you don't think God could ever change things? Are there places where the shade is too deep and the soil too poor for anything good to grow? Thankfully, it is not so. There is no place which cannot be reached by God's rainbow grace.

Dear God, forgive me for those times when I look out at my life and I think that some of it is beyond even your power to change. Deep down, I know it is not so – but I struggle to believe it all the same. Help me, today, to know that there is nothing you cannot change. Amen.

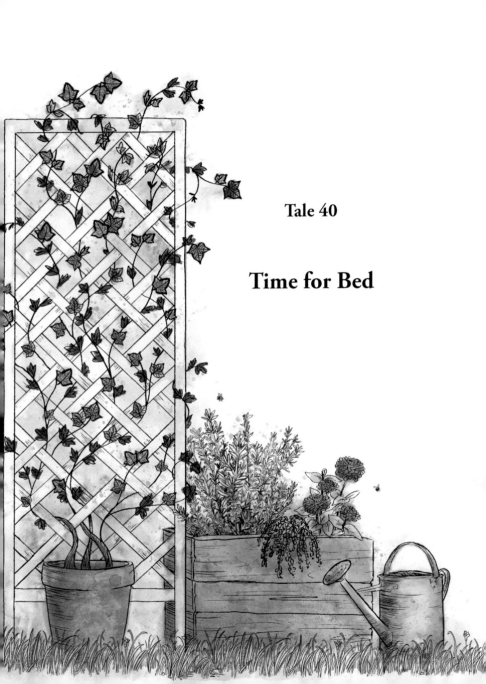

Tale 40

Time for Bed

Autumn is nearly at an end. It is the last week of November, and the weather alternates between days of beguilingly warm sunshine and days of bitter cold. It is as if the season is reluctant to leave and be on her way. Today, I have been working in the garden under a frowning, leaden sky. The last of the leaves have been raked up and packed down into their chicken wire enclosure to break down for next year's leaf mould. The last proud stems of the dahlia have been trimmed down to a few centimetres above the ground and tucked into a bed of warming, protective mulch. The last, straggling begonias, blackened now by early frost, have gone into the compost, and their planters are left lopsided now – with ivy trailing from just one end. Flowerbeds to the left and right have been lightly weeded and nestle now under a blanket of bark chippings to shut out the light and cold until warmer days should come.

And that is just the point – those warmer days will come. I have always known it to be true, of course. From early childhood we learn that the seasons turn, and that winter (with trees and presents) is followed by spring (with Easter eggs) and summer (with holidays and water fights), then back to autumn (with piles of leaves to kick and conkers to collect). That particular clock ticks and tocks inside each of us. My time in the garden has changed two things about it, though.

The first is that I hear that clock more loudly. Invested as I am in the things I have planted, I look out at the signs of seasons changing with new eyes. I look to see when the autumn winds get stronger and tie in the climbers on the fences. As they get stronger still, potted plants with taller stems get moved closer into the protective shelter of the house. When the first frosts come, I notice it not just because I don my dreaded hat for walking the dog but because it signals the end of the tender bedding plants for the year. When spring begins to warm up the soil, I notice it not just because the hat goes away but because the bulbs are thrusting up through the soil. And when summer comes, I start to not just look at the soil but to feel it, judging where the water is needed most. All of this is new to me.

However, it is not just noticing which is new, but also caring. With the change of each season comes an anticipation of what the next one will bring. For the first time last year I grew some flowers from seed, and the astonishment when it worked was tremendous. Not only that, but I started to not just buy but harvest seeds for next year's planting. On the back of my kitchen door, I have a set of twelve pockets, one for each month. As I look at it now, the pockets for March, April and May are bulging with seed packets. Some are shiny ones from the shops, others are handwritten envelopes from the garden. I wonder what crops they will yield?

Bible Reflection on Lamentations 3:22,23

Lamentations, probably written by the prophet Jeremiah, is not a portion of the Bible often visited. Let's be honest, the title hardly encourages a casual 'drop-in' for a morsel of encouragement. All the same, there *is* encouragement to be had here – about the promise of the new.

> Because of the LORD's great love we are not consumed, for his compassions never fail. They are new every morning; great is your faithfulness.

If God's compassions come new every morning, then they are worth anticipating every night – no matter how long that night may be.

Pause for Prayer

Are there plans and projects, dreams and aspirations that you have left with God for him to wake them up? Does it feel as if many winters and springs have gone by since you left them with him? Today would be a good day to name them again and to express your trust in him.

Dear God, you know how I long to see these plans come good. It seems like many new mornings have come and gone with no change that I can see. Help my patience to stretch just a little longer today, I pray. Amen.

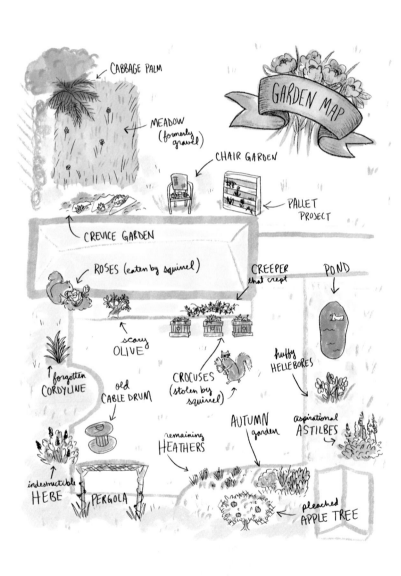

CABBAGE PALM

MEADOW
(formerly
gravel)

GARDEN MAP

CHAIR GARDEN

PALLET
PROJECT

CREVICE GARDEN

ROSES (eaten by squirrel)

CREEPER
that crept

POND

scary
OLIVE

↑ forgotten
CORDYLINE

old
CABLE DRUM

CROCUSES
(stolen by
squirrel)

huffy
HELLEBORES

AUTUMN
garden

aspirational
ASTILBES

remaining
HEATHERS

indestructible
HEBE

PERGOLA

pleached
APPLE TREE

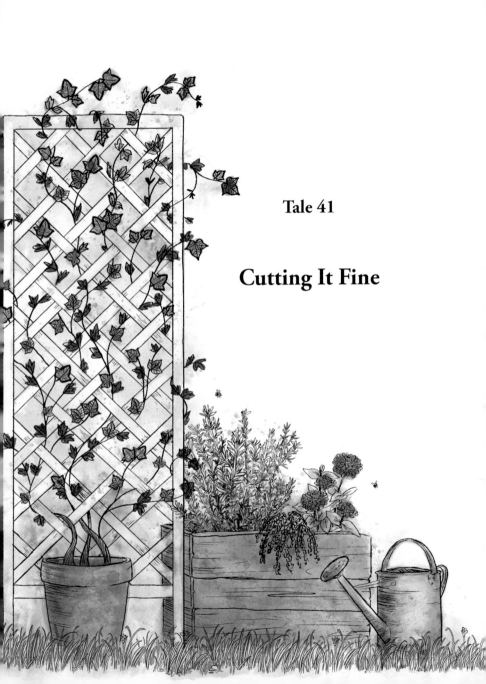

Tale 41

Cutting It Fine

Taking cuttings is not the kind of thing I do. Taking cuttings is the kind of thing that serious gardeners do. They are the sort of people who talk about 'propagating' and 'potting on' with a knowing look in their eye. Cuttings were my maternal grandfather's forte. We never visited a formal garden without him whipping out a penknife and surreptitiously slipping a cutting into the pocket of his jacket. Nine times out of ten they would take, too. Now I am about to attempt a cutting of my own and find myself hoping that some gardening gene has slipped down the generations before me.

Before I do so, though, I should introduce you to the aeonium. The aeonium is a native of the Canary Islands and is a child's drawing of a plant – with an obvious stem and a set of coloured leaves radiating like petals. They are also referred to as tree houseleeks – since, unlike their houseleek cousins, their woody stem lifts the fleshy leaves above the ground. I have two. There is a 'Sunburst', whose leaves have a lemon-yellow streak down the centre graduating into a soft green before ending in a glowing pink all around the edge. I also have a 'Zwartkop', whose magnificent shiny leaves are in a shade of burgundy so dark as to be almost black. I acquired them in a plant sale on my local allotment last summer and planted them in an old Belfast sink at the front of the house. All through the summer and autumn they gave such pleasure, with their confident, upturned faces. Winter is their growth season, and the two of them are now growing so fast that they are almost jostling for position in their little home. It is time to attempt my first-ever cuttings.

This is why the secateurs have come out. I have read, reread and read again the instructions on what to do. I have bought horticultural grit and compost to mix up for them. I have plant pots ready to go. I have kitchen paper spread out on the window ledge ready to lay the cuttings down for a day or two so that the ends can harden off a little before planting. All the same, that moment of severing the 10 centimetre-long cuttings from the main stem is a moment of agony. What if I compromise the whole plant? What if my attempt to give them more room ends up with me creating lots more room by killing them off? Where is Granddad and his magical penknife when I need him?

Cutting back in order to grow is counterintuitive, always, in every field. We can never quite believe that the one will lead to the other – and yet it is so. There are many times in my Christian life when I have mourned the loss of this or that fruitful enterprise, only to discover that it was making room for something better or more fruitful. All the same, I never seem to learn.

Bible Reflection on John 15:1–4

On the night of his betrayal and arrest, Jesus took a walk with his disciples after their meal in the upper room. On their way out of the city to the Mount of Olives, they would have passed under one of the great city gates of Jerusalem. Carved on its lintel, high above their heads, would have been a vine – its healthy leaves and plump grapes a symbol of all God's aspirations for a fruitful people. Pausing in the Garden of Gethsemane, Jesus speaks of the vine:

> I am the true vine, and my Father is the gardener. He cuts off every branch in me that bears no fruit, while every branch that does bear fruit he prunes so that it will be even more fruitful. You are already clean because of the word I have spoken to you. Remain in me, as I also remain in you. No branch can bear fruit by itself; it must remain in the vine. Neither can you bear fruit unless you remain in me.

As we have noted before, to entrust ourselves to the hands of God as disciples is to trust him with the whole business of pruning and trimming and cutting and uprooting, that his garden might grow. This is the nature of faith. It is also the place where faith and risk sit closest to one another.

Pause for Prayer

If God asked you now to give up something, even something precious, how would that feel? If he asked you to let go of something good and strong and fruitful in order that something even better might come, would you believe him? It can be a hard thing to do, but in the end, it is born out of our trust in him.

> Dear God, I know that you can see the mixture of doubt and faith in me right now. I know that letting go of what I have can never be a risk when you don't let go of me. Today, I ask you to help me believe that just a little more. Amen.

Tale 42

Lightbulb Moment

In the autumn of my first full year of gardening, I had started to notice a change in the garden centres. By this stage I was a frequent visitor, and so any changes were obvious. The change consisted of tubs and hoppers of what looked like onions. Keen (and knowledgeable) gardeners were gathering round them with brown paper bags, like children at a pick-and-mix sweet counter. They were, of course, bulbs. People were poring over them as they filled their little bags, doubtless picturing the colour and spectacle which these papery things would bring in the spring. Feeling that I had nothing to lose, I decided to try my hand at growing some. I chose a selection of daffodils and tulips. The latter were all chosen for the most striking colours I could find. Like any novice, I went home and followed the planting instructions to the letter. After that, I waited.

When the first green shoots started to come up through the compost and push aside the layer of grit on top of the pot, I was so excited. When the tulips began to unfurl in all their geometric brilliance, I was amazed. They lasted until the beginning of summer and were cheerful and surprising companions whenever I stopped for a cup of coffee outside. With the tulips especially, there was a kind of sculptural quality to them as well as all the colour. They really were magnificent.

When at last they lost their flowers, I moved the pots to the bottom of the garden, as there was no longer anything to see. Every time I passed by, I was so tempted to snip off the green stems with their browning remainders of the flowers. Every time, I resisted. Heads wiser than mine told me that the bulb hidden beneath the soil would need all the nutrients it could get from those leaves as they slowly died away. It was hard to accept, as they looked so untidy.

However, I am glad I followed the advice. Around Christmas, I took a look at the pots and those confident green shoots were thrusting up again – as if they had simply been asleep. I have moved them back closer to the house now, so that I can see how they grow and change almost by the day. Just at a time when the very last of summer's annuals are blackened by the frost, these tulips are making preparations to greet the spring. On days when the cold makes my cheeks sting every time I go to the compost heap with peelings, they are reaching out to greet the first rays of spring sunshine whenever they should come.

This is nothing short of the miracle of growth – whether in the garden or the church. From the dormant reminders of last year's faded growth, the harbingers of next year's colour begin to emerge. Some of the most colourful and vibrant voices of faith in the Old Testament come from the times of the exile, when God's people were far from home and suffering. Out of that collective winter of hardship come voices of faith and hope – like the first green shoots to embrace God's spring.

Bible Reflection on Isaiah 9:2–6

I was never a fan of learning grammar at school. In fact, I only learned in any formal way about English grammar by learning the complexities of German grammar. All the same, it is worth noting the tense used by the prophet Isaiah in this passage, so familiar from many a carol service:

> The people walking in darkness have seen a great light; on those living in the land of deep darkness a light has dawned. You have enlarged the nation and increased their joy; they rejoice before you as people rejoice at the harvest, as warriors rejoice when dividing the plunder. For as in the day of Midian's defeat, you have shattered the yoke that burdens them, the bar across their shoulders, the rod of their oppressor. Every warrior's boot used in battle and every garment rolled in blood will be destined for burning, will be fuel for the fire. For to us a child is born, to us a son is given, and the government will be on his shoulders. And he will be called Wonderful Counsellor, Mighty God, Everlasting Father, Prince of Peace.

Isaiah uses the present perfect tense here, as if the light had *already* shone in darkness and the nation had *already* enlarged its borders. In fact, neither were true at the time. Isaiah's was a voice raised during a period of profound sorrow and darkness, with the people living a wretched life in exile. So sure was Isaiah of the change which would come that he describes it in the perfect tense, as if it had already happened. From his winter, he reaches out for a spring yet to be seen.

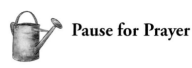 **Pause for Prayer**

Today may be a real winter's day for you on the inside. The hours of daylight may be few, and you feel cold to the bone. Today, it may be hard to imagine any kind of spring around the corner. On such days, the simplest prayer is the best one:

Dear God, please help me. Amen.

Tale 43

No Such Thing as Scrap

As you well know by now, DIY is not my forte. My father was exceptionally gifted at making things out of wood, and I inherited very little of his skill. That said, in woodwork at school I had inherited enough of an understanding to avoid outright embarrassment. In metalwork, though, it was another matter. My first-ever project was a coat hook, fashioned from two pieces of metal welded together. The screw holes in the base plate were wonky, and the hook itself was so wide that there was probably not a coat loop on earth which would have slid over it. From that, I 'progressed' to making a set of darts. I ignored my teacher's advice about not making them too heavy, as I found a bigger diameter to be easier to work on with clumsy fingers. When at last they were complete, the first dart thrown missed the cork on the board, hit the metal and bounced onto the floor, where its exceptional weight snapped the point clean off. That pretty much drew a line under metalwork for me.

Or at least it did until the summer of the desk. As you now know, the wood was removed and put to good use as a plinth for my indoor plants. This left me with a black metal frame about 1 metre across. It was too big to fit into the dustbin, and so it was propped up against the wall when my brother and his wife came to visit. They were just recently back from a trip to Albania where they had seen gorgeous displays of little pots, on metal racks, all filled to the brim with bright flowers. My sister-in-law, showing considerably more faith in me than I had in myself, suggested that I might like to try the same with the frame. I cut off the excess metal, ordered some steel wire and, when it came, set about stringing it across the frame. Both the tools I had for the job were defunct, having been bought very cheaply thirty years before. Undeterred, I ordered replacements, completed the job – and now my metal frame with its sixteen bright pots of cyclamen draws admiring gazes from passers-by.

Meanwhile, in the back garden, I undertook a long overdue job. High above the back door was a very old basketball hoop. The net was long gone, the screws had rusted and the plastic surround was bleached and cracked with age. Wobbling to the top of the stepladder, I removed it from the wall. I discarded the plastic and the shreds of the old net but could not quite bear to throw away that perfectly round metal hoop. A few days later, I painted it gold, mounted a pot in the base and started to train ivy to grow around the edges of it, softening the gold metal with its leaves and forming a new 'window frame'. My son then suggested that I might like to mount it near to the house, so that it could serve as a 'window' to the garden. I have done just that. When I look through it now, I see it differently. If I look a bit harder, I can probably see my old metalwork classroom differently too.

The Bible demonstrates again and again that our past need not define us. Moses became so much more than the adopted baby from the bulrushes. David became so much more than a giant-slayer. Paul, who had once been so keen to stamp out every vestige of Jesus, became his loyal servant. All things are possible . . .

Bible reflection 1 Timothy 1:12–17

Paul's past was ever present with him. He would forever be aware that he had judged and hounded and persecuted Christ's followers. Far from disabling him, though, it made him appreciate the power of the gospel all the more:

> I thank Christ Jesus our Lord, who has given me strength, that he considered me trustworthy, appointing me to his service. Even though I was once a blasphemer and a persecutor and a violent man, I was shown mercy because I acted in ignorance and unbelief. The grace of our Lord was poured out on me abundantly, along with the faith and love that are in Christ Jesus. Here is a trustworthy saying that deserves full acceptance: Christ Jesus came into the world to save sinners – of whom I am the worst. But for that very reason I was shown mercy so that in me, the worst of sinners, Christ Jesus might display his immense patience as an example for those who would believe in him and receive eternal life. Now to the King eternal, immortal, invisible, the only God, be honour and glory for ever and ever. Amen.

Pause for Prayer

My old primary school teacher used to say there was no such word as 'can't'. I am not sure I believe her. Mind you, I am equally sure that God can turn our lives around in remarkable ways. As you look at your life right now, are there any areas which you have written off, believing that you will never make any progress in them? Pick one to pray about now.

Dear God, you know that even to look at this makes me sad. I cannot see any way to progress here. All the same, I know you are the God of miracles – so maybe we can take a look at it together. Amen.

Tale 44

Spring Loading

It is Christmas Day 2020, and most of the country is in lockdown. For many it will be a horribly quiet affair, unable to gather with those they love and with their only contact by phone or video call. After a week of almost relentless rain, everywhere is bathed in winter sunshine. There is a heavy frost dusting the dark purple leaves of the heucheras with white icing. The ridges chewed up in the lawn by the canine racetrack are mini-mountain ridges now – sharp underfoot and capped with white peaks. The last of the summer's begonias are blackened by this harsh onset of winter and bound for the compost heap.

As I walk round the garden, though, I spot a quiet revolution. The Virginia creeper, so magnificent in the summer, is now just a skeleton of twigs and branches. On closer inspection, though, every branch, at every junction, has a tight red bud, no bigger than a pinprick, beginning to swell. My little rescued acer with its powdery grey bark is still defying the odds, and there are hints of buds there too. In my woodland garden, the remains of my astilbes are a reminder of the summer's ill-advised planting, and even the reliable tiarellas seem to have shrunk from the cold. Behind them, though, are bright green shoots of the bulbs coming through. Their tiny shoots of lime green look almost as if they were illuminated under the deep shade of the trees. I did not plant them, but they do not need me anyway.

There is something blissful about the unknowing of the garden today. These shrubs, plants and bulbs are blissfully ignorant of the world beyond the garden. They do not know about the deaths and separations. They are untroubled by the graphs and mortality rates. They neither shrink from a virus nor quiver with anticipation of a vaccine. They do the one thing for which they were created – they grow. Like an old, reliable clock, their growth cycle just spins around out of sight and turns the hands of the seasons. Today, I thank God for them.

As those who live in the world, Christians cannot be untroubled or unmoved by its plight. We 'rejoice with those who rejoice; mourn with those who mourn' (Rom. 12:15). However, buried deep down in our root system is another imperative, from another place. Paul calls it the 'upward call of God in Christ Jesus' (Phil. 3:14, NKJV). It means that even when it is the harshest of winters outside, it may be spring for the soul. Even if it is winter within the soul, there is an innate knowledge that spring is on its way.

Bible Reflection on Job 19:23–27

Job may well be the oldest book of the Bible. It certainly talks about the earliest events in the story of Planet Earth, when the 'morning stars sang for joy' at its creation. It is a hard read, though. In it a good man loses just about everything. He is tried, tested, battered and oppressed in every way. His personal winter is the harshest imaginable, and yet beneath the frozen surface lies a bulb of faith with its inbuilt clock still ticking.

> Oh, that my words were recorded, that they were written on a scroll, that they were inscribed with an iron tool on lead, or engraved in rock for ever! I know that my redeemer lives, and that in the end he will stand on the earth. And after my skin has been destroyed, yet in my flesh I will see God; I myself will see him with my own eyes – I, and not another. How my heart yearns within me!

Job is not without longing here. He is desperate for someone, anyone, to know about his plight. Through it all, though, comes the siren call of faith and the belief that God is watching.

Pause for Prayer

Perhaps it is winter for you today. Perhaps you feel as if the harshness of life makes you feel like resting a little longer, or hiding a little deeper, or sighing a little louder. That's OK, and God will be less troubled by it than you will. Maybe today would be a good day to remember, though, that heavenly clock ticking within.

Dear God, remind me today, I pray, that dead and dormant are two different things. Remind me today that heaven's seed is planted deep within me and will flower when the time is right. Amen.

Tale 45

Blissful Ignorance

This is not a good thing, I know, but I am probably prouder than I ought to be. Not to put too fine a point on it, I hate to feel stupid. Given that my parents were such meticulous and skilful gardeners and that I did not begin 'project garden' until I was half way through my fifties, the scope for ignorance was high. My knowledge of plant identification and nurture was close to zero, especially in comparison to theirs. However, since embarking on this project, I have found that my ignorance really is bliss. It means that things which other gardeners take for granted are still joyous discoveries to me.

So, for instance, when I was digging up my gravel to make the meadow, I was fascinated by the ugly tuber-type thing which I discovered lying beneath the weed-proof membrane. As you now know, I reached out to gardening friends on social media, who quickly identified it as a cyclamen rhizome. They suggested I plant it at the foot of a tree – and they were right. Having planted it in the summer, by the following winter it had gorgeous mottled leaves and flowers of scarlet and pink. This was a revelation to me.

Then there was the time when I found two or three bright green spikes thrusting up through the soil in places where I had not seen them before. As the weeks went by, they seemed to have a cluster of green berries at the top. Whatever could they be? Again, a more experienced gardener came to my aid and explained that they were lords-and-ladies. Sure enough, when the 'berries' turned a deep orange I recognised them as something which I had seen in the woods on walks with my father years before.

As you will have read in 'The Creeper That Crept', I was very sceptical that anything which looked so fragile and lifeless could ever fill the space for which I had planted it. To see one, then two, then hundreds of tiny red buds unfurl into leaves was a great joy. The journey continues to this day. I am now in January of my third year with 'project garden', and I have come indoors amazed by what I have seen. Down towards the bottom of the garden, near the shed, tiny rosettes are pushing up through the chilly soil. Each is tightly wrapped, like a miniature Brussels sprout. Whatever could they be? A fellow gardener, looking at a photo of these tiny visitors, pronounced that they were sedum seedlings. This is especially pleasing, as I have not planted them, but I know that sedums fare very well elsewhere in the garden. I am also secretly pleased that they are not Brussels sprouts, but that is another story.

The sense that there is always more to discover is what keeps the edge to this project for me. There are always new species to discover and new skills in tending old species too. Until the time should come when I can no longer do this, I shall never cease to learn – and that is a good thing. In truth, it is a good thing in our spiritual lives too. I came to faith as a teenager, and in my early years of belief, I felt very threatened by any aspect of it which seemed less than certain. Ambiguity and uncertainty were enemies, not friends. I find that is less the case now. Every time that God takes me by surprise, I am grateful for it, and every one of those occasions gives me reason to believe that there is more to come.

Bible Reflection on Philippians 3:7–14

The apostle Paul was a very knowledgeable man. Anyone who wished to train as a rabbi would have been picked from dozens of hopefuls. From amongst those who were then picked, only those with the greatest aptitude and application would have gone through. Paul had been through all of that and more besides, and yet he still had plenty to learn. Writing from his prison cell to the Christians in Philippi, he looks back at what has been and anticipates what is to come:

> But whatever were gains to me I now consider loss for the sake of Christ. What is more, I consider everything a loss because of the surpassing worth of knowing Christ Jesus my Lord, for whose sake I have lost all things. I consider them garbage, that I may gain Christ and be found in him, not having a righteousness of my own that comes from the law, but that which is through faith in Christ – the righteousness that comes from God on the basis of faith. I want to know Christ – yes, to know the power of his resurrection and participation in his sufferings, becoming like him in his death, and so, somehow, attaining to the resurrection from the dead. Not that I have already obtained all this, or have already arrived at my goal, but I press on to take hold of that for which Christ Jesus took hold of me. Brothers and sisters, I do not consider myself yet to have taken hold of it. But one thing I do:

forgetting what is behind and straining towards what is ahead, I press on towards the goal to win the prize for which God has called me heavenwards in Christ Jesus.

Like a flower leaning towards the sun, Paul reaches forward for all that is to come.

Pause for Prayer

Think for a moment of those things which still puzzle you about the ways of God. It might be the niggle of an unanswered prayer, or a quizzical sense of wonder about something he has made. Choose just one of them today and dwell on it for a few moments in his presence.

Dear God, you know this thing niggles me. Some days I get so irritated that I don't know the answer, and others, it doesn't really seem to matter that much. Let today be one of those days. Today, I want to thank you for all the things I don't understand – and trust you with them. Amen.

Tale 46

A Cut Too Far?

When I invited you to push open the gate and join me in the garden, I warned you that there would be both success and failure in these pages. I said there would be the tale of plants which flourished but others which perished. Sadly, it is time for the latter now. It is just about three weeks since I took a deep breath and took cuttings from my beloved, glossy aeonium. The story is told in 'Cutting It Fine'. I followed all the instructions to the letter, choosing the time of year, the angle of the cut and the medium for the new cuttings, to ensure success. To date, the cuttings have indeed been successful. There is one of them in the dining room now. It is standing up straight, the leaves are glossy and it is turning its pleasing round face to the light coming in through the window.

For the parent plant, though, it is a different story. In the few days following the cutting, the colour began to drain from the top leaves. A few days after that, they began to drop – leaving a forlorn little carpet around the base of the pot. The main trunk, once so strong, is now bending over as if the effort of standing up is simply too much. What have I done? I have now removed the rest of the wilting leaves and moved the plant to the shelter of the cold frame for the rest of the winter. It sits there now in the company of numerous other alpines which are sitting out the cold months. Right now, I have no idea whether it will live to see the spring.

In terms of pure maths, I shall still be winning out even if I lose the parent plant. There will still be two where once there was only one. All the same, there will be some regrets about losing such a beautiful specimen. The jury is still out on whether that will happen. Maybe I have caught it just in time by moving it to the shelter of the cold frame. Maybe I shall learn some lessons about plant care as I nurse it back to health by moving it slowly out into the sunshine when the time comes. Either way, I shall learn something!

These past couple of years in the garden have taught me that pride, as well as plants, must weather the storms. That aeonium brought me considerable pride and joy. It was placed at the front of the house, just under the main window, and often caught admiring glances from people visiting. If it has gone now because I tried to make more of it, then so be it. To try to do so was neither wrong nor without value. I shall know next time . . .

Often churches can be ironically unforgiving places when it comes to failure. Of course, they believe the gospel of love and forgiveness with all their hearts. The trouble is that it all matters so much that we feel it must be done right, or best, every single time. When that doesn't happen and a plan falls apart, it can be hard to take. Maybe I shall need to remember my aeonium next time that happens.

Bible Reflection on Acts 16:6–10

The apostle Paul was a man on a mission. On the day when he was given back his sight, he was charged with the task of taking the gospel to the Gentiles. This he did, with all his might and intellect, racking up mile after mile by land and sea. In Acts 16, he and his companions have been travelling throughout Asia Minor when they seem to run into opposition. That opposition, though, is coming from an unexpected source:

> Paul and his companions travelled throughout the region of Phrygia and Galatia, having been kept by the Holy Spirit from preaching the word in the province of Asia. When they came to the border of Mysia, they tried to enter Bithynia, but the Spirit of Jesus would not allow them to. So they passed by Mysia and went down to Troas. During the night Paul had a vision of a man of Macedonia standing and begging him, 'Come over to Macedonia and help us.' After Paul had seen the vision, we got ready at once to leave for Macedonia, concluding that God had called us to preach the gospel to them.

Have you noticed who stopped them? On the first occasion it was the 'Holy Spirit' and the second it was the 'Spirit of Jesus'. Preaching the gospel is a good thing, and yet in those places on those occasions, God kept them from doing it. Sometimes a plan fails because God has another one.

Pause for Prayer

If you stop for a moment now, can you see some of your favourite plans which just haven't worked out? Maybe they have wilted, like my plant, or gone altogether. Whichever one is most precious to you, bring it to mind right now, so that you can talk to God about it.

Dear God, I thought this was such a good idea. I thought I would enjoy it and you would smile upon it. Somehow, though, it just never happened. Help me now to hand it back to you and to see what's next. Amen.

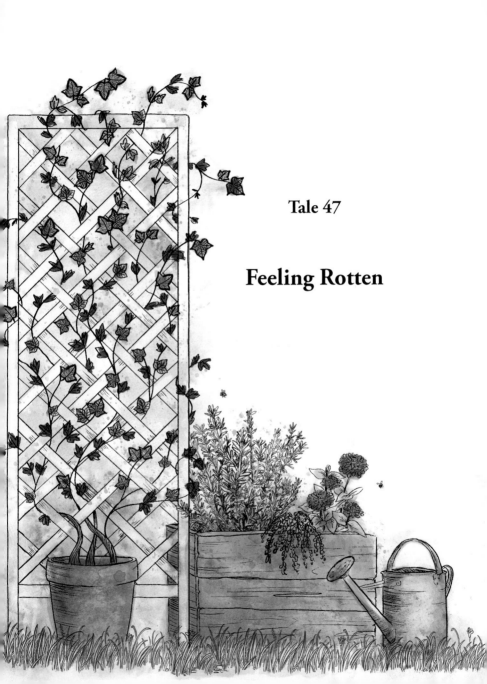

Tale 47

Feeling Rotten

'Put it on the compost heap' is a phrase with which I was very familiar as a child. That compost heap was just a few steps from the back door, and depositing fruit peelings or old salad leaves onto it was second nature. I may have thought that all my school friends did it too, though that was probably not the case. Tipping things onto it was as far as my involvement went, and the business of turning, sifting and distributing was left to my father. It clearly worked, as plants both great and small seemed to flourish under his care.

When I tackled that first flowerbed on the day when 'project garden' began, there was an old water butt at the corner of the shed. When it was covered by weeds and brambles, it didn't seem to matter. However, once the bed was cleared and planted with things I actually wanted to look at, the old water butt became an eyesore. I removed it, cut off one end to use as a planter and used the rest as a compost bin. I was terribly pleased with this act of courageous DIY, and it appeared to work beautifully. The pleasure lasted only until the next year, when I found that I could not access the compost except by lifting the whole thing up. This resulted in all the compost spilling out across the ground, when I maybe wanted just a spadeful or two.

At this point, I decided to try making use of forklift pallets again. My previous attempt to turn one into a planter had been successful, so I decided to try another project. I shamelessly scrounged three of them from a business on the local industrial estate and made them into a substantial compost bin built against the side of my decking. There is access through the top to deposit things and a gate which swings open for turning and removing the finished product. Maybe it is because I made it myself, but I find the whole thing inordinately pleasing. There is a huge satisfaction, too, to mulching a newly planted shrub with home-made compost. It feels as if it closes a circle, somehow. There have been moments too when I have caught myself looking at the labels on vegetables bought from the supermarket. How amazing that the tips trimmed from my Guatemalan green beans should help my dahlias in Berkshire to grow! In the process of saving and rotting these trimmings, nothing goes to waste.

Time spent in the garden has made me more and more aware of the interdependence which exists in nature. One plant may provide shade for another, whilst another sheds its leaves to enrich the soil for its neighbour. Plants and worms and bees and trees and hedgehogs all work together in some complex harmony which requires little or no input from me. Such is the brilliance of God's creative plan.

So often, of necessity, our view of God's actions is restricted to those which affect us and those near to us. However, the idea of sovereignty means that his plans may affect tens of millions of people all at once. Not only that, but those plans may be intricately interwoven with each other, like strands on a spider's web.

Bible Reflection on Romans 8:28–30

We talked in the last chapter about Paul's broad mission to take the gospel to the Gentile world. The journey was far from smooth – with many setbacks and frustrations as well as downright opposition along the way. Consider this description of God's sovereignty, though:

> And we know that in all things God works for the good of those who love him, who have been called according to his purpose. For those God foreknew he also predestined to be conformed to the image of his Son, that he might be the firstborn among many brothers and sisters. And those he predestined, he also called; those he called, he also justified; those he justified, he also glorified.

In working 'for the good of those who love him', God may overlap and interweave the plans of many individuals.

Pause for Prayer

If you have a minute, get a blank piece of paper and a pen and draw a
timeline of the past few years of your life. Mark the highs and the lows
and maybe even some parts where you feel you deviated from the way
you thought things would go.

> Dear God, as I hold this in my hands just now, it's hard to believe
> that every little bit of it was meant to be this way. All the same, I
> trust you – and I want to say right now that all things are in your
> hands. Amen.

Tale 48

The Indestructible Hebe

You will know from reading 'Richard the Under-gardener' that my gardening escapades in other gardens have not been glorious ones. In my previous house, the most radical thing I did was to dig up the pocket handkerchief of a lawn and replace it with membrane and gravel. The job proved much harder than I thought, as it was necessary to dig down further than expected. Not only that, but this very small space seemed to swallow bag after bag after bag of gravel. I reached the point where I almost felt my car could drive to the builder's merchant by itself!

Once the job was done, we felt that we needed to do something to 'dress' the bare patch of gravel. At a country fair we bought three green glazed pots, in ascending size. In them we planted a berberis, some trailing ivy, one or two annuals and a hebe. The hebe was in the middle-sized pot. They looked quite elegant grouped in the middle of the gravel. Not only that, but their maintenance was minimal. All I had to do was trim them occasionally and replace the annuals each year. However, it turned out that I was not the problem.

That particular house stood on the crossroads of a fairly busy road, and that was the danger. I was out buying the last bits of shopping for a big family gathering when one of my sons rang me up. He explained that a car had come through the front wall, was leaking petrol, that all the emergency services had been summoned and could I please come home. By the time I got there, all the emergency services had arrived, and thankfully nobody was hurt. There were bricks scattered as far as the front door, and the garden wall had a very large hole in it. One of the pots was gone.

A couple of years later, after the wall had been rebuilt, the same thing happened again. I was summoned home to discover a car wedged in the wall, its hazard lights blinking forlornly on and off. Many hours later, it was gone – and in the morning we started to clear up the mess. Another of the pots was gone, and now only the one with the hebe remained. When we moved to the current house, it came with us in the van. Once I started working on the garden, I relegated it from the decking to the far end of the garden as it was well past its best. It was straggly and patchy and looked to be just clinging on. In the early autumn, I trimmed it right back, thinking that might well be the last thing I did for it. Thankfully, I was wrong. It is now growing back healthily again. This little shrub, which has repulsed two car attacks, is now fighting back. I might just have to move it closer to the house, I think!

Although my role as a pastor is to care for others, I am continually inspired and strengthened by the example which they set me. Time and time again, I have seen them in the direst of circumstances rallying with courage and faith. I have lost count of the number of times I have walked away from a hospital bed, glowing from an encounter with inextinguishable faith.

Bible Reflection on Daniel 3:16–18

We tend to associate the book of Daniel with the story of the lions' den. However, Daniel is not the only one in that book showing considerable courage. His three fellow captives, Shadrach, Meshach and Abednego, also have to stand up for their faith. Refusing to bow down to a pagan idol, they say the following:

> King Nebuchadnezzar, we do not need to defend ourselves before you in this matter. If we are thrown into the blazing furnace, the God we serve is able to deliver us from it, and he will deliver us from Your Majesty's hand. But even if he does not, we want you to know, Your Majesty, that we will not serve your gods or worship the image of gold you have set up.

It is worth noting that their courage and faith are resolute, no matter what the outcome may be.

Pause for Prayer

Today is a good day to thank God for someone whose example inspires you. Think of someone whose courage or perseverance has reminded you that God is near.

Dear God, I thank you for this person today. I thank you that they have shown such resilience and courage when times are tough. Help me to do that when my time may come, I pray. Amen.

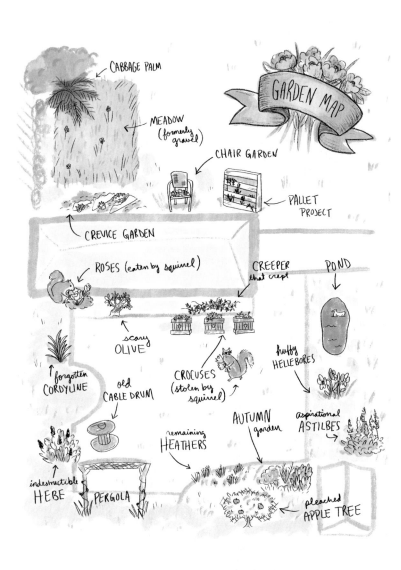

CABBAGE PALM

MEADOW
(formerly
gravel)

GARDEN MAP

CHAIR GARDEN

PALLET
PROJECT

CREVICE GARDEN

ROSES (eaten by squirrel)

CREEPER
that crept

POND

scary
OLIVE

huffy
HELLEBORES

↑ forgotten
CORDYLINE

old
CABLE DRUM

CROCUSES
(stolen by
squirrel) ↑

remaining
HEATHERS

AUTUMN
garden

aspirational
ASTILBES

indestructible
HEBE

PERGOLA

pleached
APPLE TREE

Tale 49

An Excess of Inspiration

It's rather childish, I know, but the sound of post clattering through the letter box has always given me a frisson of excitement. Of course, it may well turn out to be something as unpleasant as a bill or as mundane as a pizza leaflet – but there is always the possibility that it could be something else. Now into my third year of 'project garden', something else has started to land on my mat in the very early part of the year. They are thick and glossy and full of ideas – the seed catalogues. In them are pages and pages of full-colour photos showing the kind of blooms which would make any gardener's heart swell with pride.

I know the idea is that I should look through them, look out of my window and instantly be inspired to carpet my garden with a sea of colour. In truth, though, that is not quite how it goes. Instead, my mind goes back to the late spring of my second year in 'project garden'. By this stage, I had started to buy a gardening magazine or two, and often they would come with free packets of seeds. Not having a greenhouse, I waited until later in the year when they could be safely sown outdoors. I gathered up a selection of trays and pots, lined them with membrane and scattered on a handful of spare gravel before topping up with good compost. This is where my mistakes began.

My first was to ignore all the instructions about spacing the seeds out and sowing them sparingly. After all, I reasoned, with my lack of experience they were unlikely to thrive anyway – so why not maximise my chances? Of course, it did the opposite. Those which did come up were all too close together and started to choke each other out. My second mistake was to throw away the details of what was in which tray. This meant that when I came to the next stage of pricking them out and transplanting them to the garden, I did not know what was what. The tall flowers intended for the cottage garden went into the hymnbook shelf on the pew instead, and the short ones were planted in the garden. Any blooms which did result were more by luck than judgement, and the finished result was a very long way from the pictures in the seed catalogues.

Of course, I shall probably try again – but neither hopes nor expectations are high. Sometimes we carry our disappointments with us like shackles which hobble us every time we try to move forwards. The fact that we have got something wrong does not have to mean that we shall make that mistake again. If anything, it will make us less likely to do so.

Maybe the next time a seed catalogue falls onto the mat, I shall open it. This time, I might even follow the instructions on the seed packet.

Bible Reflection on Isaiah 40:27–31

When Isaiah was at the height of his powers, the people around him were in the depths of despair. They had been brought up on tales of God's great acts of the past, but now they struggled to believe them any more. In this passage, he rallies their hopes once again:

> Why do you complain, Jacob? Why do you say, Israel, 'My way is hidden from the LORD; my cause is disregarded by my God'? Do you not know? Have you not heard? The LORD is the everlasting God, the Creator of the ends of the earth. He will not grow tired or weary, and his understanding no one can fathom. He gives strength to the weary and increases the power of the weak. Even youths grow tired and weary, and young men stumble and fall; but those who hope in the LORD will renew their strength. They will soar on wings like eagles; they will run and not grow weary, they will walk and not be faint.

I read these words and it makes me believe that no one is a lost cause to God. With him, as Jesus himself would go on to say 'all things are possible' (Matt. 19:26).

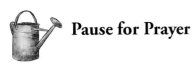

Pause for Prayer

Is there a project on which you have given up altogether? Do you feel that you have failed with it so many times that it is simply not worth trying again? It is just possible that God may have other ideas . . .

Dear God, you know how I feel about this. You know the dark cloud of defeat which settles about me every time I think of it. As I offer it to you once again now, bring both clarity and courage, I pray. Amen.

Tale 50

Twisted and Beautiful

This being my third year in 'project garden', one of my Christmas presents had been a garden centre voucher from my mum. When the time came to head off to a newly reopened garden centre nearby, I had no clear notion of what I was looking for. The only thing in my mind was that I wanted it to be 'significant'. I wanted to buy something that I could plant and every time I caught sight of it, I would feel as if it were an emissary from someone I loved. The garden centre in question has large buildings and an even larger outdoor space. With my rattly trolley and its squeaky wheel, I made my way up and down between the benches, admiring all the plants. Occasionally, I would bump over a watering hose with an almighty clatter, turning heads in every direction. This was proving not to be a simple trip.

I was starting to head back in towards the centre with a largely empty trolley when I spotted them. There were four or five of them on the end of a bench, and they caught my eye instantly. Their twisted limbs reminded me of something out of a fairy tale where the hero of the story would brave an enchanted forest on his travels. They were *Corylus avellana* 'Contorta', or twisted hazel. Apparently, they are also known as Harry Lauder's walking stick, though I shall stick to their more ordinary name. In winter time, their twisted, corkscrewing branches are on display for all to see. Come the spring, there will be golden catkins too, but it is really the branches which caught my eye. If I were to stop now and look out of the window, I could spend a lot of time tracing the path of each one and admiring how they twist and turn around each other. Their beauty is in their complexity, and every twist adds to the intrigue.

Sometimes we pine for the simple life, as if it would solve all our problems. The truth is that, since many of our problems are within, it would probably not. Not only that, but it is often in both complexity and adversity that the true beauty of character and faith are to be seen. Time and time again, I have seen people's faith flourish precisely at that moment when life's course fails to run true. In the twists and turns there is beauty, strength and reserves of faith which they never thought were there. I have a feeling that my twisted hazel will get more intriguing the bigger and older it grows. I believe the same could be said of faith.

Bible Reflection on Daniel 4:34–37

The exciting parts of the book of Daniel that most people remember are Daniel surviving the lions' den and his four friends surviving the fiery furnace. However, they are not the only ones to go through such trials. King Nebuchadnezzar was an exceptionally arrogant ruler, with his name inscribed on every fourth brick of the great city of Babylon. He believed himself to be greater than God and only changed his mind after a severe trial:

> At the end of that time, I, Nebuchadnezzar, raised my eyes towards heaven, and my sanity was restored. Then I praised the Most High; I honoured and glorified him who lives for ever. His dominion is an eternal dominion; his kingdom endures from generation to generation. All the peoples of the earth are regarded as nothing. He does as he pleases with the powers of heaven and the peoples of the earth. No one can hold back his hand or say to him: 'What have you done?' At the same time that my sanity was restored, my honour and splendour were returned to me for the glory of my kingdom. My advisors and nobles sought me out, and I was restored to my throne and became even greater than before. Now I, Nebuchadnezzar, praise and exalt and glorify the King of heaven, because everything he does is right and all his ways are just. And those who walk in pride he is able to humble.

This was a harsh way for a king to learn such a lesson, but learn it he did. Built into the twists and turns of his life now was an awareness of the greatness of God.

Pause for Prayer

Try to close your eyes for a moment and look at the twists and turns of your life, as I look at my hazel tree. Some of them may seem to have a purpose, whilst others leave you puzzled. Could it be that God is in there somewhere, even in the most unexpected twists?

Dear God, today I confess that my life looks awfully messy from here. Some of the twists and turns make sense, but others simply don't. Right now, I pray for the ability to believe that you were in it all, at all times. Amen.

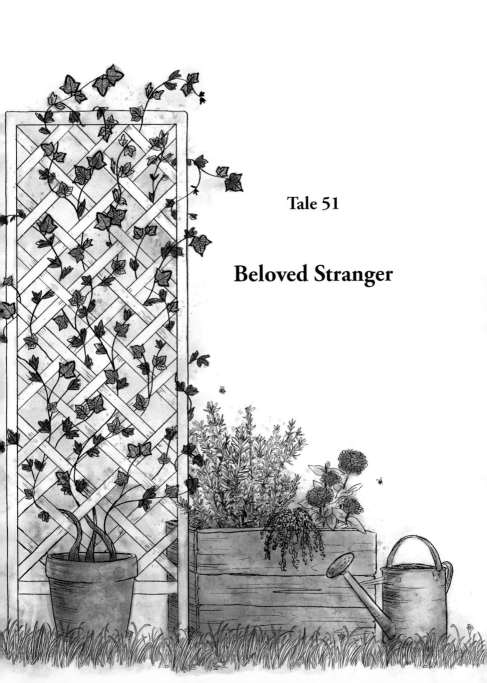

Tale 51

Beloved Stranger

In retrospect, the combination of enthusiasm, ignorance and rock-bottom bargains was probably not a good one. My local garden centre was in the last few hours of its sale. Indoors, there were empty shelves to the right and left and others which had been partly dismantled. As people picked over the bargains, the things which were left got more and more untidy. Outside, it was even worse. People were rummaging through plants, knocking them over and doing their best to beat each other to the bargains. I had at least one plant stolen 'accidentally' from my trolley and had to ask for it back! My trolley was almost full when I spotted one enormous, spectacular plant lying on its side. It was clearly not in the right place, as it was somewhere between a palm and a fern, but was in amongst the small bedding plants.

The plant had two strong trunks, looking like a palm tree, and a profusion of spectacular sword-like leaves in emerald with yellow edging. I didn't know what it was or where it belonged, but I felt inclined to rescue it from such an ignominious end. When I got to the till, it turned out that nobody there knew what it was either. They asked each other, called for the supervisor and, in the end, made an educated guess. Although established plants of that size seemed to be in the £40–50 range, they were uncertain, so decided to charge me £5.

With some difficulty, I brought my treasure home, and then scratched my head about where to put it. At this stage, I had not really started work on the front garden, but there was plenty of room. I cleared a corner in the gravel, sunk a good, deep hole and planted this enormous new stranger as carefully as I could. So far as I can tell, it is a cordyline (or cabbage palm). Whatever it is, it does not really fit where I have put it. Above it is a Portuguese laurel tree, beside it are some small lavenders and in front of it now is my meadow. A palm which looks as if it belongs on the promenade of a seaside town does not really fit in that corner. And yet, it is happy and thriving. Not only that, but I am happy too. My palm takes very little looking after, apart from occasionally removing dead leaves from the bottom. It has withstood all the upheaval of me removing the old gravel from round about it and digging up the soil with mattock and shovel (a story which you will have read in 'From Gravel to Glorious'). It has tolerated heavy rain, falling leaves and even snowfall. Through it all, it gazes across the meadow at me now, and I look back at it. Whatever a planting plan or gardening guide may appear to say to the contrary, it belongs there. Rescued from a shabby end, it appears to be enjoying its questionable new home.

Bible Reflection on Colossians 1:19–23

The apostle Paul did not really belong. His relationship to the Christian church had begun as a sworn enemy of all who followed Jesus Christ. In later years, he never lost his sense of privilege at what it meant to be included in this way:

> For God was pleased to have all his fullness dwell in him, and through him to reconcile to himself all things, whether things on earth or things in heaven, by making peace through his blood, shed on the cross. Once you were alienated from God and were enemies in your minds because of your evil behaviour. But now he has reconciled you by Christ's physical body through death to present you holy in his sight, without blemish and free from accusation – if you continue in your faith, established and firm, and do not move from the hope held out in the gospel. This is the gospel that you heard and that has been proclaimed to every creature under heaven, and of which I, Paul, have become a servant.

God is in the business of welcoming those who don't deserve to be there, as every Christian man and woman can testify.

Pause for Prayer

Do you know anyone who feels as if they don't belong? Do you know someone who wants to fit in but just can't quite seem to manage it? Maybe you could help to change that for them.

Dear God, I thank you today for the welcome you have given me. Thank you for accepting me into your family with generosity and grace. I pray for this particular person today, that they might feel those things too. Amen.

Tale 52

Not My Garden

It happens every time. Whenever I answer a set of questions on a phone survey or similar, they will ask me whether or not I own the property. 'No,' comes back the answer. So then they ask me whether I rent it, and again the answer comes back as 'no'. At that point, they run out of boxes to fill in on their form and the conversation generally tails off. I live in that old-fashioned thing, tied accommodation. My house (and garden) are provided to me by the church whom I serve. When I cease to work as the church's minister, both house and garden will cease to be mine.

Sometimes, especially when I have laboured to the point of a stiff back on weeding a reluctant flowerbed, a pang of melancholy comes over me. 'All this,' I think, 'and someone else will live with the fruits of these labours.' I feel it even more when I see the shrubs which I planted in the first year of tending the garden getting bigger and bigger. When they are fully established, their shapes round and full and their flowers cascading down the sides, it will be somebody else who admires and tends them. It is an odd feeling.

In reality, though, all sense of permanent possession is an illusion. Even if we live in a house which we own outright, with a garden which we can rightly call our own, it will not be ours for ever. If we have planted trees, especially, they will outlive us by many years. Their roots will be feeling their way through the damp earth and their branches brushing the far sky long after we have moved on. We are temporary stewards of the garden, temporary guardians of the earth, only for so long.

One day, in the providence of God, I shall move on from this garden. Somebody else will watch as the sun moves on from the left-hand fence, slices the bottom fence in two at midday and then bathes the right-hand fence in the golden glow of evening. Somebody else will see if the clematis survives another year or the Virginia creeper succeeds with its attempt to swallow the decking whole. They will watch the frogs come and go in the pond and savour the swishing of the meadow grass in a summer's breeze. It will be their garden then, at least for a while – just as it has been mine for a while too.

Out there, with the wind in the trees making the leaves sing above my head, I often think of Moses standing on the edge of Mount Nebo. Stretched out before him was the dazzling sight of the Promised Land, just as it had been described of old (Deut. 32:49). It must have been an awkward moment, since God had to tell him that he would see it but not occupy it. The plan would go on, but he would not.

Of course, there is nothing of the patriarch about me, but a man can dream . . .

Bible Reflection on James 4:13–15

So far, I have resisted having a garden planner – although it is only a matter of time. I do, however, have a fabric planter with twelve pockets in it hanging on the back of a door – as I have mentioned elsewhere in this book. When I buy seeds, or harvest them, I put them in there so I know which month to plant them. I suppose it is a planner without the words or the pen. The thing is, though, there are so many things I don't know. The twelve months represented by my little pockets might bring torrential storms or terrible drought, for all I know. Gardening is a seasonally repeated lesson in humility.

Let's read the words of James the apostle as he dishes out advice to some people in the early church:

> Now listen, you who say, 'Today or tomorrow we will go to this or that city, spend a year there, carry on business and make money.' Why, you do not even know what will happen tomorrow. What is your life? You are a mist that appears for a little while and then vanishes. Instead, you ought to say, 'If it is the Lord's will, we will live and do this or that.'

Pause for Prayer

What is that area of life where you find it hardest to accept that you are not in charge? It is sure to be more important than my garden – it is probably something to do with family, friends or work. Why not spread it out before God, a bit like the Promised Land spread out in front of Moses, and tell him all about it?

Dear God, sometimes I feel so little and this thing seems so big. Every once in a while, it feels like there is nothing I can do about it. Remind me again, today, that all things are in your hands. Amen.

Guerrilla Gardening

The whole world began with a garden, though no human hand ever planted it. We shall never know, because the words of Genesis never furnish us the details, how exactly that planting took place. Did the words of God cause oak trees to rush full-grown from the earth, I wonder? Was there an audible hiss as more than 300,000 plant species began to nudge tentatively through the soil? Part of the joy of gardening is the sense of gradual revelation. A bulb or a seed is but the ugly harbinger of beauty and colour yet to come. As we saw in our chapter 'Planting Now for Then', things may be planted seasons, or even years ahead of when they are expected to reach their full impact.

When I was a teenager, I had a bit of a thing for adding badges to my jacket. Other people did it with CND badges or the logos of their favourite rock bands. One of mine had a child's drawing of the world on it and a question in spidery handwriting:

Dear God, when you made the world and the stars and the planets and everything – did you have a project book?

I loved the naïve innocence of the question and still do. I wonder if he did have a book? What we do know is that this was the first, and maybe the last, time that a garden was brought forth from the earth by speech alone. In the words of Genesis 1:11,12, it all sounds beguilingly easy:

> Then God said, 'Let the land produce vegetation: seed-bearing plants and trees on the land that bear fruit with seed in it, according to their various kinds.' And it was so. The land produced vegetation: plants bearing seed according to their kinds and trees bearing fruit with seed in it according to their kinds. And God saw that it was good.

I would love to know whether the tallest trees came first and then the ground cover seeped in underneath them. Or maybe it all started at the bottom and grew upwards, starting with moss and tiny alpines, reaching at last to the cloud-scraping wonder of a giant sequoia. Perhaps all the colours came at once, like a Jackson Pollock canvas of global proportions – with spatters of fuchsia pink, lemon yellow and deepest blue in no particular order. Or perhaps there was a sort of 'Mexican wave' of colour gradually encircling the planet, as yellow gave way to orange which yielded to peach, which blushed to pink and so on? These are pleasant mysteries on which to ponder.

However the job was done, we do know that God's first task as gardener was to hand over this newly planted wonder to the care of Adam and Eve. We are given no indication of how long they had to peacefully enjoy it. We don't know how many days they spent brushing past the grasses and flowers, wistfully naming them as they went. As a novice gardener, I still struggle to get my head around the complexities of Latin classifications when it comes to naming plants. However, I take great delight in their less formal names, like snapdragon, Granny's bonnet or foxglove. Adam and Eve must have had such fun with the naming. We don't know how many evenings they spent looking up through the trees at the darkening sky and counting the stars above their heads. Of course, they had no unplanted wilderness with which to compare their jewel of a garden. To them, the earth had always been like this. It would not last, though.

This idyllic existence in their perfect garden was coming to an end. All it would take was a lie, a theft and an attempt at deception, and the whole thing would fall apart. Significantly, though, it was not just their corner of the earth, the planted paradise of Eden, which would suffer:

> To Adam he said, 'Because you listened to your wife and ate fruit from the tree about which I commanded you, "You must not eat from it," cursed is the ground because of you; through painful toil you will eat food from it all the days of your life. It will produce thorns and thistles for you, and you will eat the plants of the field. By the sweat of your brow you will eat your food until you return to the ground, since from it you were taken; for dust you are and to dust you will return.'
>
> *Genesis 3:17–19*

In these words, we learn that not only was Eden closed to them, but also that the rest of the planet was affected too. From that moment onwards, planet Earth would yield flower and fruit only after a struggle. 'Thorns and thistles' would interrupt every bid to cultivate the land. And so it has been ever since. Every attempt at horticulture, from a vast arable collective on the American plains to a window box in Hackney, must battle the scourge of weeds. To grow things of our choice, in a chosen place, is to join battle with a creative order whose job is now to fight back.

Every time we take a patch of earth, no matter how large or small, and seek to make it produce the plants that we have chosen, this is an act of rebellion against the consequences of the Fall. Every thorn from pruning a rose and every resurgence of ground elder after you think you have dug out the root is a reminder that cultivation is a battle. Against the odds, we strive to make a patch of God's earth better than it was before and to impose our mark upon it. A couple of years ago, I had the privilege of touring one of Britain's great country estates with the man responsible for managing it. He is a lovely Christian man, with a keen sense of Christian calling to his work. On our tour round the vast estate, we paused at a forest where some clearing and thinning was under way. Maybe seeing my shock at the pyres of burning wood, he noted that forestry management was all about the future. He went on to explain that the fruits of what was happening that day might be seen in sixty or seventy years' time. 'I want to leave the earth better than I found it,' he said.

Somebody asked me recently why I don't get an allotment to give even more vent to my gardening bug. As a novice to gardening, I feel it would be to overreach myself. I have enough problems keeping on top of the weeds in one patch, let alone two! However, it is not just a question of effort or time. There is something more profound than that. For now, it is especially important to me to transform the patch of ground where

I am living. I want to look out of a window and see that I have made a tangible difference to my patch. I want to look and see that in one garden, or even in one corner of one garden, I have taken on the challenge issued to my forefather Adam to make a go of the earth and somehow make it better. So long as I have so much to learn, that enterprise will take all my gardening skill to effect the transformation.

Of course, it is not only the land which is transformed. In the act of preparing, cultivating, planting and tending a patch of God's earth, we are transformed too. A friend of mine, who has followed 'project garden' from afar, commented on what she had seen in it. 'What enriches a garden enriches a soul,' she said. How true that is. If we talk about this as a struggle, then it is well known that the harshest adversity brings out depths of strength and ingenuity of which the human race can be proud. In short, it does us good. This is one of the reasons that horticulture has been so much a part of the penal system in the past two centuries. Those whose lives have gone wrong, for whatever reason, can make something go right in the earth at their fingertips. For those who feel that life has done things to them, this is an opportunity to be the actor in their own story – to make something good happen in the space around them of which they can be rightly proud. Not only that, but the kind of nurture which most plants require is relatively simple – and yet they quietly yield the benefits of fruit and flower, texture and fragrance, to those who will tend them.

Part way through my second year in 'project garden', I paid a visit to the City of New York. I would not really describe myself as a 'city person', but I loved it. I loved the crazy juxtapositions of old and new. I loved the studied elegance of art deco architecture. I loved the sparkle on the waters of the East River. I was also very taken with the city's green spaces, both great and small. It would be hard not to be impressed with the majestic landscape of Central Park, especially when I visited in the autumn. However, there are hundreds of other green spaces, ranging from squares and boulevards to neatly tended flowerbeds in the central reservation of busy highways. What I did not know at the time was that many of them are tended by 'graduates' of the Horticultural Society of New York's 'GreenHouse project'.[3] Under the scheme, those who learn how to care for plants and to tend the earth in prisons such as Rikers Island can join the city's garden workforce as interns on release. Both the city and their lives are flourishing as a result.

Gardening in the context of the earth after Eden can be an almighty struggle from which good things come. It is not, of course, something which you can ever 'finish'. Until the earth stops spinning, the cultivation of its surface will be a constant battle with the weeds born of the Fall. Not only that, but as the earth spins, so the seasons turn and the challenges become different in autumn, winter, spring and summer. In autumn, there is lots of maintenance to be done, so that autumn leaves don't choke smaller plants as they bury them. In winter, tender plants must be protected from the frost and others mulched for their hibernation until the spring. When spring comes, a flurry of planting must be preceded by a flurry of weeding, since the weeds, too, are in the process of waking up. Summer brings the challenges of heat and decisions about which plants to water, when and in what way. The challenge of the garden is the challenge to the gardener, season by season. Those who would have a garden with colour year-round can do it – but they must plan, plant and labour to make it so.

The late Steve Jobs was one of the richest and most influential inventors of his age. His technology is probably used in every continent on earth. He drove a revolution in both technology and design, which has never stopped. He is often quoted as saying that he wanted to 'put a ding in the universe'[4] – at which he surely succeeded before his untimely death. Along the way, he inspired many others, both young and old, to do the same. My garden is a very small corner of a very small planet in a very big universe – but it is a ding nonetheless.

Longing for the Trees

I was not a very good Scout. I was hopeless at knots, my uniform was rarely pristine and I lacked the competitive spirit which caused the other members of my troop to fill the arm of their shirt with proficiency badges of every kind. I do remember the games, though, and one in particular. It went something like this – everybody would sit in a circle, and the first player would say, 'When I go to heaven, in my rucksack I will take . . .'. Each new participant would then add to the growing list, and the memory challenge would grow harder and harder as it went round the circle. What would I take to heaven if I could, though?

I sometimes wonder whether I would take my beloved hori-hori trowel or at least a good pair of gardening gloves. There's a pair of really sharp secateurs it would be hard to leave behind, too. After all, as we saw in 'God the Gardener', we are promised that at the very least there will be trees in heaven – so maybe there will be plants too. If that is the case, then surely somebody will need to look after them. Surely even heaven's trees will need an occasional prune, or the weeds teased out from between their roots. Then again, with every last vestige of the Fall removed, maybe there would be no pruning required and no weeds to dig up with my trowel.

The point is actually slightly more serious than it sounds. Part of the fulfilment for any gardener is precisely the fact that it takes place in the context of adversity. Gardeners reserve a special kind of respect for those who bring forth gardens of great beauty and intrigue in unforgiving circumstances. Those who make a vertiginous slope sing with colourful planting or those who make the desert bloom are a source of both respect and envy. When I look out on my garden now, far from perfect as it is, my greatest pleasure comes from knowing how much better it is than it was before. The act of transformation is where the true joy is to be found. In pitting both body and wits against the sometimes uncooperative earth, I feel as if I am fulfilling some of my calling as a human and an earth-keeper.

If there are to be living plants in heaven, who will tend them? Of course, if they grow by themselves with neither pests nor weeds to oppose them, then no tending will be necessary. Personally, I find that a shame. Most human beings, at some level or other, thrive on challenge. Devoting mind, heart and body to achieve something against the odds is part of what makes us gloriously human and reflects the image of God. Change is thrilling, and all the more so when you help to bring it about. Perhaps our perfected selves will not need such things, though, and will find full contentment in the perfection all around us. I have to say that I cannot imagine it. Then again, the only equipment I have for my imagining is the mind and heart I have in this life right now.

If there are to be gardens or orchards in heaven, I hope God will allow us the joy of caring for them. Not everyone will want to, of course.

Last summer, someone asked me whether I would not just like to sit back and look at the garden I have created. The answer at the time was both yes and no. From time to time I love to sit back and admire it. I enjoy that, especially on a summer morning with a coffee in hand when the water is splashing in the pond, the birds are busy in the trees and the nodding head of a sunflower grown from seed is moving with the lightest of breezes. Coffee drained, though, I am as likely as not to get up, leave the mug behind and don my gardening gloves. There is always something to prune, a weed to pull up or a dead head to snip off. Later, when the sun has set, there is always a new project to plan or ideas needed about some new corner to tackle. The joy is in the unfinished nature of the task.

I hope that there will be gardens in heaven where I can labour for the pleasure of the one who planted them, and for my own pleasure too. From time to time, I shall look up from the weeding, pleased that others enjoy the scents and colours as they go about their business. For those others, I hope there are libraries crammed with unread stories and laboratories fermenting with new discoveries of wonder. I hope there are oceans to cross and mountains to climb and an infinity of possibilities. When their journeys are done and their stories read and their discoveries savoured, I hope there will be a garden in which to sit and watch the sun go down. I think there probably will be.

Notes

[1] D.H.S. Nicholson and A.H.E. Lee, eds, *The Oxford Book of English Mystical Verse* (Oxford: The Clarendon Press, 1917).

[2] Melissa Harrison, *Autumn* (London: Elliott & Thompson, 2016).

[3] https://www.thehort.org/programs/greenhouse/ (accessed 25 February 2021).

[4] Original source unknown, although the quote can be widely found on the internet.

Bibliography

Allaway, Zia, ed., *RHS What to Plant Where* (London: DK, 2013).

Don, Monty, *Down to Earth* (London: DK, 2017).

Dock, Katie, and Fiona Wild, eds. *RHS How to Garden* (London: DK, 2005).

Harrison, Melissa, *Autumn* (London: Elliott & Thompson, 2016).

Spence, Ian, *RHS Gardening Month by Month* (London: DK, 2007).

Stuart-Smith, Sue, *The Well Gardened Mind* (London: William Collins, 2020).

Titchmarsh, Alan, *How to Be a Gardener: Back to Basics* (book one) (London: BBC, 2002).

Titchmarsh, Alan, *How to Be a Gardener: Secrets of Success* (book two) (London: BBC, 2003).

37 Kings and a Budgerigar

*Advent reflections inspired by
nativity sets from around the world*

Richard Littledale

For many of us, putting out a crib set is one of our treasured
Christmas traditions. But what do these scenes really tell us about
the original nativity story?

Join Richard Littledale as he shares reflections, Bible readings
and prayers for each day of advent based on his own personal
collection of nativity sets from around the world.

Renew the wonder of the Christmas story through these thought-
provoking devotions.

978-1-78893-158-8

Postcards from the Land of Grief

Comfort for the journey through loss towards hope

Richard Littledale

Losing a loved one can be a lonely, isolating and disorientating experience. Written as postcards from this land of grief, Richard Littledale honestly shares his personal experience in an accessible way that helps fellow travellers to identify their feelings and find hope in the foreign country of bereavement.

Thought-provoking, honest, gentle and ultimately hope-filled, this is a helpful companion for anyone dealing with loss.

978-1-78893-071-0

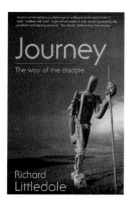

Journey

The way of the disciple

Richard Littledale

'I want people to consider their life's journey, wherever their feet might take them, as a pilgrim's way – complete with leaving home, provisions, communications, distractions and a journey's end.'

In this delightful book, Richard Littledale helps us relate the concerns of the pilgrim's life to our own, and how this practice can help us walk a God-guided path. Enriched by the writings and artwork of other pilgrims, you'll be drawn along the trail, meet fellow travellers, have time for reflection, and find yourself changed by the journey.

978-1-84227-985-4

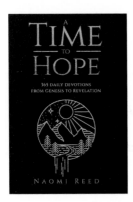

A Time to Hope

*365 daily devotions from
Genesis to Revelation*

Naomi Reed

Many of us have favourite Bible verses that we draw comfort
from, but we don't always know their context or understand how
they fit into the main story arc of the Bible.

Tracing the big picture of God's story through the key themes and
events from Genesis to Revelation allows us to see the abundant
riches in God's Word. As you read the unfolding story day by
day, you can encounter God in all his glorious holiness and
faithfulness.

If you have ever struggled to read the Bible from cover to cover,
then this devotional will help you find a way in to God's big story
and help you fall in love with Jesus all over again.

978-1-78893-144-1

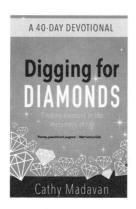

Digging for Diamonds

A 40-day devotional

Cathy Madavan

In this 40-day devotional based on the bestselling book *Digging for Diamonds*, Cathy Madavan encourages us to discover more of the life-transforming treasures of our identity, strength, character and purpose that God has already placed within us.

Each day includes a Bible reading, a devotional thought, questions for reflection and a prayer.

Spend 40 days digging for diamonds and find the treasure hidden in the messiness of life.

978-1-78893-152-6

30 Days with Ruth

*A devotional journey with
the loyal widow*

Emily Owen

What must it have been like to be Ruth, transformed from a
widow in a foreign land to become the great-grandmother of King
David?

Emily Owen explores these questions through Ruth's 'diary',
sharing in her trials, her excitements, her challenges, fears and
joys. Each chapter begins with a 'diary extract' from Ruth's
life, which is then beautifully unpacked with a meditation
to encourage you to reflect on how that applies today. Each
meditation is encouraging yet challenging and helpful for personal
growth.

Join Ruth on a devotional journey to see the biblical story from a
fresh perspective.

978-1-78893-179-3

God Speaks

40 letters from the Father's heart

Ruth O'Reilly-Smith

Ruth O'Reilly helps us to slow down, listen to God and respond to him in this beautiful devotional journal.

God speaks. If we take the time to quiet our racing thoughts and be still for a moment, we can hear him. He is speaking all the time.

Draw closer to God as you listen to 40 messages of love straight from the Father's heart, reflect on Bible verses and learn to talk to God with guided questions and prayers. As you write your thoughts in the journaling space provided, you will create a precious record of how God speaks to you that you can always treasure.

Deepen your walk with God as you listen and respond to him speaking to you in this beautiful devotional journal.

978-1-78893-222-6

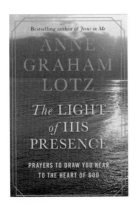

The Light of His Presence

Prayers to draw you near to the heart of God

Anne Graham Lotz

Like many of us, Anne Graham Lotz has struggled with prayer. Over the years, she discovered that writing out her prayers draws her into deeper, more intimate conversations with God.

The Light of His Presence offers forty of these tender, honest prayers for real-life situations as an invitation to deepen your own prayer life through worship, confession, thanksgiving, and intercession. You'll be encouraged to lean more fully into God's promises through this power-packed devotional resource, which includes inspiring quotes from Christians throughout the ages and also has space to journal your own words to God.

As Anne writes, "My prayer for you . . . is that God will use my struggle with prayer to help you overcome yours. And that, as a result, you will be drawn nearer to the heart of God."

978-1-78893-204-2

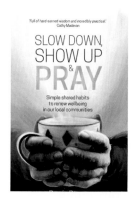

Slow Down, Show Up & Pray

Simple shared habits to renew wellbeing in our local communities

Ruth Rice

How can we renew wellbeing in our own lives and in our local communities?

Looking after our mental health has never been so important. Many of us want to find simple ways to help our wellbeing that we can fit into our everyday life.

After suffering her own mental health crisis, Ruth Rice set up the Renew Wellbeing charity, which helps churches open safe spaces to help all attend to their mental and emotional health. Packed full of personal stories, reflective resources and practical guidance, this book will enable you to maintain your own wellbeing and encourage churches to provide Renew spaces that help local communities journey alongside each other to renew wellbeing.

Be present. Be prayerful. Be in partnership.

978-1-78893-183-0

Authentic

We trust you enjoyed reading this book
from Authentic. If you want to be
informed of any new titles from this author
and other releases you can sign up to the
Authentic newsletter by scanning below:

Online:
authenticmedia.co.uk

Follow us: